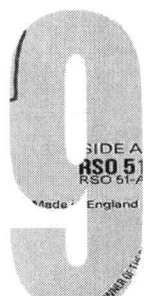

IN 1979 AND 1980

TONY CHARLES
POUK HILL PRESS

JANUARY 1979

4th: Don's diary started the year with a rather inglorious entry:

He was up very early and went by cab to the local Magistrates Court to face prosecution on his drink-driving charge. The judge was not interested in his 'excuses' for not being able to taste or smell the alcohol and banned him from driving for a year and fined him £120.

He went to a local pub for the rest of the day.

> **That Don Powell of Slade (of whom we don't hear so much these days — Nostalgic Ed) was fined £130 for drinking and driving in a Hampstead court last week?**

6th: Don's diary stated that he was at home, waiting for an engineer to come to fix his phone line, and spent the day watching various television programmes.

A recent incorrect internet rumour had Slade down as playing at The Star Club in Hamburg on this date.

8th: Don helped out at Advision with recordings for Nick Van Eede.

9th: Rehearsals, The Lafayette, Wolverhampton.

10th: Rehearsals, The Lafayette, Wolverhampton.

11th: Rehearsals at a school hall in Wednesbury.

12th: Rehearsals at a school hall in Wednesbury.

13th:
Don did a fan club interview (reproduced below).

18th:
Meeting with accountant Colin Newman to sort their tax situation out and to form a limited company for the group.

24th:
The group listened to the rehearsal tapes. They then visited Portland Studio, but they couldn't record anything there as the technicians were still putting the new control room together. Meeting with Colin Newman to discuss a possible new record deal.

25th:
Meeting with Colin Newman re tax.

Then the group headed off to Portland Studios to record two songs, one of which was 'Not Tonight Josephine'.

26th: Portland Studios - overdubs.

30th: A story in the Daily Mirror.(right)

WHY NODDY FEARS GROUPIES

GIRL fans, groupies who follow pop stars everywhere, are part of the legend of rock and roll.

As Slade prepare for a British tour in spring, lead singer Noddy Holder hopes not to meet anyone like the 18-year-old Puerto Rican who put him through a nightmare on the band's last tour of America.

The girl, who had followed the band around America, broke into Noddy's hotel room in New York, and locked herself in the bathroom.

Blood

Noddy explained: 'What I saw when I broke the door down was absolutely terrifying.

'She had slashed her wrists with a knife, and blood was pouring to the floor.

'I really thought she was going to die. I called the hotel manager and we got a doctor right away.

'I didn't expect to see her ever again, but after a couple of weeks there she was at all our concerts once again, and there she would be in the hotel bar. It still gives me the shivers.

'The funny thing was she never spoke to me—either before or after the incident.'

The Fan Club had interviewed Don Powell at his home for the January / February newsletter.

Q: Don, what do you think of playing the nightclub dates, rather than the concert halls, when you go on the road again?

A: Well, it's the best thing really. Because we were away for so long in the States, we couldn't really expect to go back to the big concert halls, because we wouldn't fill them. So we went back to doing small places – we know we could fill those and thus start to build ourselves up again.

Q: Have you made a lot of fans through the nightclub dates?

A: Well, what has happened really is that certain nights there have been much older crowds, and people have come up and said they used to follow us five years ago. They even mention places we played, and I don't remember half of them! Then they have to rush off to get back to look after their kids!

Q: Which audiences would you say were the best, the Southern ones, or the Northern ones?

A: It's hard to say really, as far as I'm concerned it's all the same. Obviously in certain areas there are different songs the audiences like, but as far as saying which is the best, say South or North, I don't see how you can really answer that.

Q: Are you aware of what the audience reaction is like when you are playing?

A: Personally, myself, not really. I can't see much, and I can't hear a lot, because the guitars are so loud – but I can maybe see a few things when the lights go up, and I can see out into the audience, otherwise I can't see anything.

Q: At Reading University on the last tour there was a crash barrier and it started to collapse, and nobody seemed to notice.

A: You'll find that those crash barriers cause more problems than what they were made to stop. Even when there are bouncers down the front, if they weren't there, I'm sure that there would be no problems. It's when they are there that the problems are caused. There is no need for them, because Nod can handle the crowd anyway!

Q: What happened at Porthcawl though, was when Noddy told the bouncers to get lost, the fans weren't sensible enough to stand back and they all got on stage.

A: That wasn't really the kids fault. Even the particular bouncer that bopped Nod one wasn't employed by the club that night. He just took it on his own back to go down there and stand in line with the rest of them. So when Nod cleared the bouncers out of the way, he took offence, which is stupid, and he waited for Nod afterwards and bopped him.

Q: How did you feel about that yourself when it happened?

A: That was weird. We were walking round backstage and this guy came up shouting. We took no notice of him, and the next minute Nod was lying on the floor!

Q: Has Nod taken any legal action at all?

A: The bloke has been prosecuted. Nod and Chas travelled down to Porthcawl last week to press charges. He was on line, anyway, for another case to be put against him.

Q: Have you any plans for the next tour? Any new songs?

A: We will be doing some new ones. We started rehearsing this week, but it's mainly for new recording material. We go into the studio next Thursday, I think, obviously though, we will be adding new material to the live show. As far as the show goes, as yet, we don't know. We haven't really planned it.

Q: What sort of songs will be on the new album, and when will it be released?

A: Again, I can't really say. We've got a lot of stuff recorded, bit I can't really say. I don't know myself, yet!

Q: Do you plan to go abroad again soon?

A: Believe it or not, there are some plans to go back to Poland in February. Can you imagine February in Poland? It'll be about six foot deep in snow! I think there are some European dates planned. We've had dates in Germany and Scandinavia offered to us, but they are just offers. We haven't gone into them yet and had a look to see what's what.

Q: What was it like when you were in Poland last year?

A: Great. The concerts were amazing. We did eighteen shows in twenty one days. It was really funny, because a lot of them were open-air, like in big parks. I used to stand backstage watching the kids coming in. you'd see lots of Mums and Dads coming and sitting with their kids. They'd have shopping bags with them, and they'd bring out their sandwiches!

Q: Are you going back to America?

A: There's no plans at the moment, because we'd rather work in England and Europe.

It was later reported that the Polish dates were cancelled.

FEBRUARY 1979

1st: Portland Studios - recording 'Hold On To Your Hats'.

2nd: Portland Studios - mixing 'Hold On To Your Hats'.

5th: Portland Studios – Slade recorded 'Let Me Love In To You'

Thursday 15th: Romeo and Juliets. Lord Square, Blackburn.
Don's diary stated that the show was so-so and that the club's onstage equipment was lacking.

Friday 16th: Romeo and Juliets. Lord Square, Blackburn.
Don's diary reported another so-so show. £600 of damage was reported to have been done at the club on that night.

Saturday 17th: Romeo and Juliets. Lord Square, Blackburn.
After the gig, Don drove to Grimsby with the crew - to stay the night before tomorrow's gig in Cleethorpes.

Sunday 18th: Bunny's Place. Grant Street, Cleethorpes.
Support: Nick Van Eede

Monday 19th: Baileys, Haymarket, Leicester.
Support: Nick Van Eede.
Don's diary reported another so-so show.

Tuesday 20th: Baileys, Haymarket, Leicester.
Support: Nick Van Eede

Wednesday 21st: Baileys, Haymarket, Leicester.
Support: Nick Van Eede
Don's diary reported that Chas Chandler and his partner attended.
Don was not particularly impressed by their show.

Thursday 22nd: Baileys, Haymarket, Leicester.
Support: Nick Van Eede
Don's diary reported a good show.

Friday 23rd: Baileys, Haymarket, Leicester.
Support: Nick Van Eede
Don's diary reported a good show.

Saturday 24th: Baileys, Haymarket, Leicester.
Support: Nick Van Eede
Noddy Holder and Don Powell went to the cinema in the afternoon to watch the new Superman film.

Sunday 25th: Baileys. The Parade, Watford.
Support: Nick Van Eede

Monday 26th: Baileys. The Parade, Watford.
Support: Nick Van Eede

Tuesday 27th: Baileys. The Parade, Watford.
Support: Nick Van Eede

Wednesday 28th: Baileys. The Parade, Watford.
Support: Nick Van Eede

MARCH 1979

Thursday 1st: Baileys. The Parade, Watford.
Support: Nick Van Eede

Friday 2nd: Baileys. The Parade, Watford.
Support: Nick Van Eede

Saturday 3rd: Baileys. The Parade, Watford.
Support: Nick Van Eede

Slade
Watford

If ever a group personifies the volatile nature of the pop game then it's Slade. For two years from 1972 they could do no wrong... had even the heaviest critics foaming at the mouth about how wonderful they were.

They had credibility with a big C. long before Jimmy Pursey was fostering his working class myths, Slade were into bad spelling in a big way — 'Take Me Bak 'Ome', 'Mama Weer All Crazee Now', 'Gudbuy T'Jane' and 'Cum On Feel The Noize'.

Only it was fun then, and however crass you thought Slade were there's no denying they could write decent chunes.

Then they blew it. Their movie *Flame* failed to ignite the public's imagination, repeated attempts "to break" Slade in America failed, and — fashionable though it was to be working class in '76 — by this time Slade were strictly outre.

Still managed by ex-Animal Chas Chandler, they're now to be found working the colleges and cabaret circuit and are regulars at Watford's Baileys. Although acutely aware of their unenviable position, they still attack with all their old gusto.

The Baileys' audience wasn't exactly bristling with life, but for all the band seemed to care they could have been bill-topping at Earl's Court.

The glitter has gone, platform boots are left in the wardrobe (though Noddy Holder still wears his trusty titfer), but the only concession to 1979 appeared to be Dave Hill's leather strides and a severe shearing of his locks.

Visually and musically they were tight and exciting. Hill and Jim Lea swopping stage positions with energetic dexterity.

In the final analysis there is little real difference between Slade and Status Quo or Thin Lizzy. And it could be that a hit single would shoot them back to the top.

But it could also be that they're designed to remain in the shade for the rest of their natural... time will tell.

Steve Clarke

Hear Me Calling / My Baby Left Me / Ginny Ginny / Take Me Bak 'Ome / Lemme Love Into You / Everday / Somethin' Else / Pistol Packin' Mama / Get Down And Get With It / You'll Never Walk Alone / Mama Weer All Crazee Now / MXE singalong: "So here it is, Good Old Watford..." / Cum On Feel The Noize / I'm A Rocker / Born To Be Wild.

Monday 5th - Hamilton Club. Henry St, Birkenhead.
Support: Nick Van Eede
Hear Me Calling / My Baby Left Me / Ginny Ginny / Take Me Bak 'Ome / Lemme Love Into You / Everday / Somethin' Else / Pistol Packin' Mama / Gudbuy T'Jane / Get Down And Get With It / Mama Weer All Crazee Now / Cum On Feel The Noize / I'm A Rocker / Born To Be Wild.

Wednesday 7th - Great Hall, Bradford University
Don's diary showed that he enjoyed the show and that the group met a couple who were getting married to the sound of Everday.

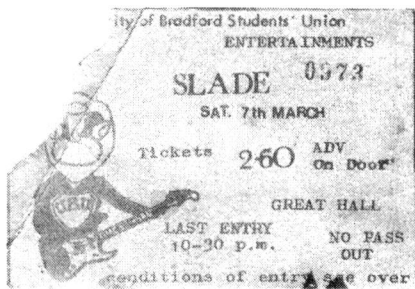
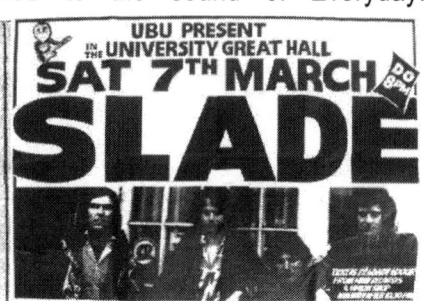

Thursday 8th - Hull University Mad March Ball.

SLADE — on stage at Hull University.   Picture Alan Park

Slade's past starts to catch up with them

SLADE—HULL UNIVERSITY

THE BIGGEST and loudest sound system I have ever seen at Hull University could not hide the fact that Slade were yesterday's heroes last night.

Vocalist Noddy Holder led the way through old classics such as Take Me Back, 'One and Every Day, but the band rapidly faded into heavy-metal cliches.

New material was shrouded in dry ice, but even the choking clouds could not hide the limits of Slade's half-hearted attempt at ska-disco music.

Their only claims to fame came at the close of the set with speeded-up versions of Gudbuy T'Jane and their first hit, Get Down and Get With It, but the nostalgia backfired.

The Top 10 hits of the early 1970's were reduced to fast throwaway versions and the band fast became caricatures of their former selves.

The crowd, thrusting fists forward and jiving to every number, did not seem to worry on the night of the Students' Union ball, but as an old Slade fan who loved their early arrogance and heavy originality, the performance was a big disappointment, for me.

An encore of the sublime Mama, Weer All Crazee Now did not help and only a smoke-ridden finale of Born To Be Wild satisfied my nostalgic urge.

Bands cannot live on past glories alone and although Slade may have more to their credit than most, it must be time that they began to lie down and accept them.—**ALAN BURGESS**.

Friday 9th - Sheffield University.
Support: JALN Band.

Saturday 10th
Barbarellas Club.
Cumberland St,
Birmingham

Don's diary reported a great show, attended by Steve Gibbons.

Don neglected to mention in his diary that Noddy Holder's favourite stage guitar had gone walkabout.

Years later, the person who took it contacted Noddy Holder to ask for his forgiveness. Noddy has said that he was less than impressed. He didn't ever get the guitar back.

Noddy loses fave axe

NODDY HOLDER of Slade has lost his favourite cherry red Gibson guitar.
Last seen in a SG/Junior case, the guitar is worth around £400 and was stolen from Slade's dressing room at Barbarella's in Birmingham last Saturday.
If anyone can help in recovering Noddy's lost prize possession, he is willing to offer a substantial reward.
Any information please to Susan Ching at Barn Records. Tel: (01) 637-2111.

147—Dancing, Discos Cabarets

barbarella's Ltd

Cumberland Street, Birmingham . B1 2JS
Tel 021 643 9413.
Friday March 9th
Tonight
THE 'SKIDS
Saturday, March 10th
SLADE
Sunday, March 11th
OCEAN BOULEVARD
Tuesday, March 13th
THE SMIRKS
Thursday, March 15th
SPLIT RIVET

15th - Portland Recording Studio, London recording Lemme Love Into Ya (then known as Let Me Give You Love).

17th - Don went to see Eddie and the Hot Rods in Aylesbury.

21st - Portland Recording Studio, London, overdubs on 'Chakeeta'.

22nd - Portland Recording Studio, London. Don's drums were set up in the toilet to do overdubs on 'Hold On To Your Hats'.

23rd - Portland Recording Studio, London.
After Slade's session in the studio, Jim and Frank Lea were recording 'When The Lights Are Out' – which would eventually be released as The Dummies. Don stayed behind to put tambourine on the track.

Slade's European dates nearly didn't happen, as Jim Lea mislaid his passport and searched high and low for it, only finding it just before the group were due to set off for the airport.

Wednesday 28th - Roes club, Lintig, Germany

The band met at Heathrow and flew to Bremen, then they drove on to Lintig. Don didn't think much of the first show. They all retired to a hotel afterwards and had drinks.

Thursday 29th - Marlborough Club - Rheindalen, Germany.
The group drove to Rheindalen and the club venue turned out to be in an Army camp. The band were offered a single room between all of them as accommodation, so they went and found a hotel instead. Don said that he enjoyed the show itself.

Friday 30th - Dancing Light Club - Wetzlar, Germany.

Saturday 31st - Diet Hmarscher Hof - Pahlude, Germany.
The band had to change hotels when they arrived as there were no bathrooms in the hotel.

APRIL 1979
Sunday 1st - Mick Mack - Baden, Germany.

Monday 2nd - Love Story, Cologne, Germany.

Tuesday 3rd - Love Story, Cologne, Germany.

Wednesday 4th – Marschweghalle, Kaltenkirche, Germany.
THE SHOW WAS CANCELLED. Don Powell said that everything was a complete shambles, so they abandoned the gig. To add to their woes, their hotel in Berlin didn't have a note of their booking, so they had to find another hotel.

Thursday 5th - Metropole - Berlin, Germany.
Jim Lea and Dave Hill went to do a radio interview.

Friday 6th - To Act - Weissenhoe, Germany.
Don reported the show as so-so.

Saturday 7th - Wartburg Music Hall, Weisbaden.

Hear Me Calling / My Baby Left Me / Take Me Bak 'Ome / Lemme Love Into Ya / Everyday / Ginny Ginny / Jim and Don solos / (gap in tape) / Get Down And Get With It / Mama Weer All Crazee Now / Cum On Feel The Noize / I'm A Rocker / Born To Be Wild.

Sunday 8th - Morgens Au Aiden - Hamm, Germany.

Monday 9th - Hyde Park - Osnabruck, Germany.

Tuesday 10th - Star Club - Hamburg, Germany.
The band's truck had broken down on its way from Bremen, but the gear did arrive in Hamburg and Don said that he enjoyed the show.

Thursday 12th - Kiel.

Friday 13th
The group travelled to Belgrade and had a three day break.

Sunday 15th – The group arrived in Yugoslavia.

Monday 16th - Unknown venue, Yugoslavia.
Don Powell did an interview afterwards.

21st – Banja Luka, Yugoslavia.
Don Powell reported that the gig was a CRAP show.

Sunday 22nd - Unknown venue, Yugoslavia.
The stage was set up in the very middle of the hall which is very unusual layout for a rock show. The attendance was not good on the night.

Monday 23rd – Unknown venue, Yugoslavia.

Tuesday 24th – drive to Austria. Unknown venue.
The group's gear was no allowed into the hall until later afternoon, so it was a bit of a race against time to get the equipment set up, and tested in time for the showtime.

Wednesday 25th – Vienna, Austria. Unknown venue.

Thursday 26th – Vienna, Austria.
Don did a radio interview, then the group drove to Lintz.

Friday 27th - Lintz – Austria.

Saturday 28th
The group flew back to England. Louise Lea met them and drove Jim and Dave back to Wolverhampton

Monday 30th
Swinn's stag night in Wolverhampton.

The Fan Club newsletter contained a Jim Lea interview, conducted backstage at one of the Watford Bailey's gigs.

Q: Jim, you've played three tours in the last year. How do you rate this one, as compared to the others?

A: We were offered to come back to do these Baileys clubs. We didn't want to do them in the first place, but we've returned and drawn twice as many people as the first time we appeared here. Playing here for a week in Watford alone, means we are going to play to 14,000 people, whereas if we did a one-nighter at the college, we would play to 1,000, even if it was sold out.

Q: What has the reaction been like on this tour?

A: You can't really count the reaction in this type of place, because the idea is to get over to people who wouldn't see us normally. So if they are sitting in the audience, they don't know anything about rock'n'roll concerts – and we're using this gig as a gig. We're not trying to be The Three Degrees. So we bring all our PA and amplifiers in and do our show. People can walk out and say it was too loud and they hated it, or they can sit there and enjoy us and hopefully get off on it at the end and go and tell their mates 'I had a great time last night. I went to see Slade.'

This is obviously what has been happening, as the audience is so much up on last time. The managers are really freaking out.

Q: Is it going to be a regular thing, playing the Baileys clubs on every tour?

A: I don't think so, but whatever way you look at it, you're playing to people. If you wanted to be a martyr to yourself you can go and play at the regular concert gig up the road, and play to only a thousand people, or however many turn up.

Q: What's the best club that you've played on this tour?

A: It depends. At Blackburn they reckoned that there were a hundred tables smashed or damaged. I mean that was a good night!

Q: On to the new album. What sort of songs will be on it?

A: It's a mixture. It's nothing like 'Whatever Happened To Slade'. I can't really say yet though, as we went into the studios for eleven days and did twelve tracks. We plan to record about twenty songs in all, then choose the best ten or eleven for the album.

Q: You seem to have returned to the old-style Slade music, rather than stay heavy, as you were with Whatever Happened To Slade'. Do you think that this has worked well?

A: Yeah. The releases after Whatever Happened To Slade' are the songs that got played on the radio, like 'My Baby Left Me', which was a near miss, but it got played on the radio, which is better than it being completely obscure, isn't it?

Q: 'Rock And Roll Bolero', which was a really catchy song, didn't do so well. Why not?

A: The comment on 'Rock And Roll Bolero' is that it was different for Slade, but it was ordinary compared to everything else that was going round at the time... But I really dig the record myself.

Q: With singles do you intend to make better B-sides, as have been on the last couple of records, rather than use a 'Don't Blame Me' type time-filler kind of song?

A: When we come to make B-sides, we don't particularly think that we have to make a strong B-side. It's just a case of using whatever tracks are going. But we're lucky in the way that every song we write has got something going for it. You could say that 'Don't Blame Me' was a time-filler. I think it was created as that. When it was used as a B-side we didn't even know it being used. It was chosen by the offices. We were in America recording the Christmas single. There was a rush to choose what to put on the back of it, and that track happened to be used.

Q: What's the reaction of the press like towards Slade now?

A: Well, a guy came in here after last night's show, who was from one of the music papers and he said that he really enjoyed the show, and that our old numbers sounded really fresh and that they could have been written yesterday. We sat there not knowing whether to believe him, because the press always tend to put barriers up against us because we haven't had a hit record for three years. If we get another couple of hits under our belts though, that will all change.

Q: Sheila Prophet was different though… she liked the group.

A: But like you said, we have gone back to doing more of the 'old' sort of thing and she's into that. You see, when we walk on stage we can rip the arse off straight rock, but we can't do the same with 'Rock And Roll Bolero'. It's a great record, but it's us thinking 'we're not being ourselves'. I was talking to this bloke the other day and he saw us in 1967, and he said that we were different to other groups even then. I asked him what he meant by 'different' and he said that we would play a Tamla Motown number, and it wouldn't be like The Four Tops, or whoever, doing it. He said other bands would play this stuff and try to get it to sound like the actual record, but we were never like that. But the thing is we were always trying to sound like the records, but when we played, it never came out like that. He said our music came out like a ton of bricks, but we never intended that!

Dave Hill was interviewed next. He did very well to put up with some of the strange questions and observations that were put to him.

Q: Dave, can you give us a run-down for your daily routine for when you play concerts like this one at Baileys tonight?

A: Well, actually with these gigs it's been a bit like a night-shift, which has completely thrown me. I reckon that I should be getting up at about two o'clock, then working here until about two o'clock in the morning – that's the time that I'll leave after the gig – getting home at about five, going to bed about that sort of time then, as I said waking up again about two o'clock. I always have eight hours sleep, you see. Certainly no less than that, maybe a bit more. It tends to throw you a bit when you do the night-shift bit because you feel strange during the day.

Q: Do you still like playing clubs like this, though, where you have got to go on stage late at night?

A: That's the only thing I don't like about night-clubs. I mean, if you're doing a normal gig, you're finished by eleven or twelve o'clock, and you'll get home by about two o'clock, and thus have a normal sort of routine. I don't like having to be in bed during the day. I'd rather be up in the morning. I'm more of a day person than a night person. I feel that it's more natural to be up during the day, whereas Nod will have a kip during the day, and it doesn't bother him. He can groove every night of the week, but I'd feel as if I was hemmed in, if all I was ever seeing was darkness. I like the 'day' routine more and I probably prefer the routine of concert gigs rather than playing clubs, but they have to be done, so I do them.

Q: At concerts though, have you ever noticed the audience, and has the way that they have reacted ever affected you, good or bad?

A: Say we have an awkward audience, like those in these clubs, where you get girls wearing pretty dresses, and women in hen parties, who have never seen a rock group, or certainly have never seen a group like us, so they just sit there... Well a lot of gigs have been like that, and we've had to work hard to get them off their seats. They don't instantly react. They're probably really liking it, but they haven't got a clue as to what they're supposed to be doing. Whereas fans like yourselves know the sort of thing that we are after every night.

So the attitude of the group is sort of 'you WILL enjoy yourselves!' We aim for having a hectic night. It's almost like playing sport – if you play squash, say, you're going to hit the ball and sweat like crazy. That's your aim on stage, to physically move yourself. Well, when I go on stage I like to move around and I like to play, and I get off on it. If I see an audience getting off on it too, then that magnetism comes back. But also if we go on stage and the audience is 'instant' from the start, then that doesn't hold us down any… it only means that we will push to do the normal show, and push to sustain the reaction.

Q: Do you prefer the concerts nowadays where you have to win the crowd over, rather than those from a few years back, where you had them with you at the start?

A: we do feel that the reaction that we get nowadays is a lot more genuine, because it simply is a lot harder to get. Obviously when you are a huge success, you are getting a lot of people in at the gigs who are just buying the odd single or two, and they've probably just come down to see what it's all about. Also they've probably heard "we shall scream at the gig" or "we shall jump around at the gig" or something. Also the crowd seems to be a lot younger at the concert gigs, so they are likely to be more clowny and loon about.

At these club dates some of the people that come in each night are fans, old fans that have grown up and are coming to see what we are about now. They probably still consider us to be something from the past. They don't know quite what they are going to get. What we do notice now is that if we do get claps that it is more genuine than the hysteria. This is one thing that will keep us together. If we are still going down well without hit records at the present time, then we know we are winning.

Q: Talking about you personally on stage, you seem to have lost a bit of your stamina, because Jim seems to have taken over. Now though you are creeping back to the way that you were before. Is this intentional, or is it just me imagining it?

A: You seem to be noticing it more than most people would. I don't know, maybe it's the clubs that are making the situation like it is. Also maybe Jim has stepped up and taken the spotlight away from me a bit, as opposed to me lowering myself. I'm not that much different, it's only you noticing Jim doing it more so, you know, moving around and that.

I would say though, that at one point I did quieten off, but not consciously. The reason for me stepping up is because it's like 'aggro' at these places. You see the audience sitting there, and you've got to project to them, some sort of image to get them going. If you're not jumping around, moving about and enjoying yourself, then they aren't going to, either.

Q: But obviously you are the real entertainer of the group.

A: I've never thought of myself as that. I've always thought of me as just being another member of the group that does what he does. Nod talks to the crowd and I muck around... Image-wise, I suppose me and Nod are the strongest, only because we come across as being the strongest on stage.

Q: When I started liking the group, you and Nod were the only ones that I knew of.

A: Right. It was my clothes that got me known!

Q: Why did you spell your song titles wrongly?

A: We didn't do it to be consciously gimmicky. We did it because that was the way that we talked, and that was the way that we would write the words, by how they sounded. This was opposed to us speaking straight English. 'Because I love you' – obviously we could say 'Coz I Luv You. This worked in our favour, so we kept on doing it. We dropped it eventually though, because it was turning into a gimmicky thing. You know, you do it once, then you do it twice, then somebody says 'Oh no, *not again!'* You have to call a halt to something before people get fed up with it.

Q: Talking about yourself, you're the sort of 'gimmick' member of the group – first you had the glitter and the platform boots, then it was the bald head and leather jacket. What's next?

A: I can't really tell you, can I? I will probably just appear with something. I don't know. I don't actually plan to do anything as such. I think that somehow going through the clubs, and through the gigs that we are doing, that I get an inspiration and I do something. I'm not particularly planning anything at the present time. The last thing that I would want to do though would be to walk on stage with glitter on, or anything of that description. I don't want anyone to look at me as being a figure of the past. I want to be NOW.

My idea has always been to look for the next craze, or to bear it in mind, anyway. I've got some new ideas for some clothes but, I'm not bringing them in yet. I can do a lot of things when we have another hit, because this will open a lot of doors for me. There is nothing worse than looking dated, so the idea is to keep trying new things and to keep the interest going.

Q: Were you ever pressed into wearing any of the old clothes by the management at all?

A: Oh no! You must be joking. Our management could never think of anything like that. Everything I do is always ME.

Q: You're more 'way-out' than the other members though, aren't you?

A: Yeah, but I was like that at school, before I met this lot! I suppose that there is something in me that the others haven't got, but that applies to each of us. Take Don. He's the quieter sort of bloke, or Jim who's really musical. Each of us is totally different and it means that we're all blended together. I don't sit here thinking that I project more than Don does, but someone will come up to me and say that I am the idiot of the group, because that's how they see me.

Q: Some people have said that you are a bit of a big head?
A: Obviously. To be aggressive or to be a performer, you have to have a certain ego, attitude. You can't ever walk onto a stage looking a bit timid, because the audience will walk all over you. They really do in America.

Q: Dave. Are you setting your intentions on getting to the top again?

A: I'd be a liar to say that we didn't want another hit record, or several. Meaning 'the top' to be the number one group, well, I think that's always in the offing as far as we're concerned. There's always a big chance that we'll do that again.

Q: When you were very big, did the pressures ever get you down?

A: Sometimes. The pressures that we've got now are enough, but we still get recognised, still get bothered. We put up with it better now, though.

Q: Would you prefer not to have instant number ones, and thus have more of a quiet life?

A: I wouldn't ignore instant number ones, no. I wouldn't say that I wouldn't strive for something like that again. Understanding more about the music industry now, it's just that the situation with the marketing of records now means that it's impossible to have any more straight to number one records. We've done it and that's the end of it as far as we're concerned. Even John Travolta, who's top of the teen mania at the moment can't achieve it.

Q: Would you like to re-live those times?

A: I wouldn't like to re-live anything. I want to have new experiences. To go through the old experience again would be boring. I want to go through success again, having more album success, and perhaps single records that are more respected. This doesn't mean that our old stuff isn't great – singles like Mama Weer All Crazee Now will always be classics in their own right.

Record Mirror printed another letter from an irate Slade fan, threatening the press with physical harm from Dave Hill if they didn't start reporting on Slade with a bit more courtesy.

> **No mercy**
>
> YOUR MUSIC biz critics better watch out because Slade, that bunch of superstars from Wolverhampton are back. Every week their legion of followers grows by leaps and bounds — soon Slade will be in the charts again. I hope that when they return to the top they will show you no mercy for your harsh comments. I'll even inform Dave Hill to get his platform boots on, so that he can stomp on your fingers till they crack. That will put a stop to you scribbling obnoxious words about the kings of rock.
> Dave Kemp, West Hamptead.

MAY 1979

Wednesday 2nd - Swinn and Debbie's wedding. The reception was held at Tenters Wine Bar.

Tuesday 8th - Recording at Portland Studio, doing overdubs.

Wednesday 9th - Dave and Don Recording at Portland Studio.

Thursday 10th - H, Jim and Don - Recording at Portland Studio.
Friday 11th - H, Jim and Don - Recording at Portland Studio, overdubs.

Saturday 12th - Colin and Meta Newman's wedding celebration.

Monday 14th - Recording at Portland Studio, doing overdubs.

Tuesday 15th - Recording at Portland Studio, doing overdubs.

Wednesday 16th - Recording at Portland Studio, doing overdubs.

Thursday 17th - The group had a business meeting at Noddy Holder's place in Chelsea. Barn had gone bankrupt.

Saturday 21st - Bedfordshire University Rag Ball. Cancelled.

Wednesday 23rd - Rehearsal, Wolverhampton

Thursday 24th - City Centre Club, Coventry

Friday 25th - Agricultural College, Tetbury Road, Cirencester.

**SLADE
Cirencester
Agricultural College**

Slade on the second date of their Spring tour played at the May Ball of the Cirencester Agricultural College. The gig took place in a huge Marquee tent, similar to a circus big-top, and the 2,000 or so crowd of students were treated to sets by the Young Bucks and the Show Stoppers before the main act appeared.
The audience pushed forward to the front of the stage as Noddy Holder started Slade's act with the opening guitar riffs to *Hear Me Calling*. Even at this point you could see that the crowd were intoxicated enough to make it a good rocking evening!
Slade continued with more old favourites. *Take Me Bak 'Ome* and *My Baby Left Me*, before introducing their new single *Ginny Ginny*, which went down as well as the preceding numbers, proving it to be a good choice for release.
Slade's music was tight, energetic and loud (very) and the lighting was perfect.
More oldies such as *Mama We're All Crazee Now*, *Gudbuy T' Jane*, along with some excellent new Holder/ Lea compositions. The best new song being *Let Me Give You Love*, an eerie number, with superb solo guitar work by Dave Hill.
On reflection Slade did seem to play too many of their old hits, but they were what the audience wanted, so they had to play them! During the encores though a fan climbed up one of the poles supporting the tent, causing the roof to drop a good 15 feet. Noddy Holder was laughing so much that he found it hard to continue. Anyway this concert proved one thing, Slade brought the roof down, and 1979 could well be their year. **Dave Kemp, West Hampstead.**

SLADE CUM BAK (again!)

Slade (remember them?) are making a come-back with an album, single and tour. The wild midlands group have a single released on May 25 entitled *Jinny, Jinny*. Like all their previous hits, it is written by Noddy Holder and bassist/violinist Jimmy Lee. It comes out on yellow vinyl.
They have been working on a new album which will be released later this summer—when they will undertake a tour.

Barn release the single Ginny Ginny / Dizzy Mama on BARN002.

Again, Slade released a high quality single that seemed to be pretty much unbeatable. Both sides were excellent, catchy songs. It was just as good, if not better, than anything on the singles charts.

They put it on coloured vinyl, which buyers sought out at the time.

This had to be THE ONE. Did buyers seek it out?
It appears not.

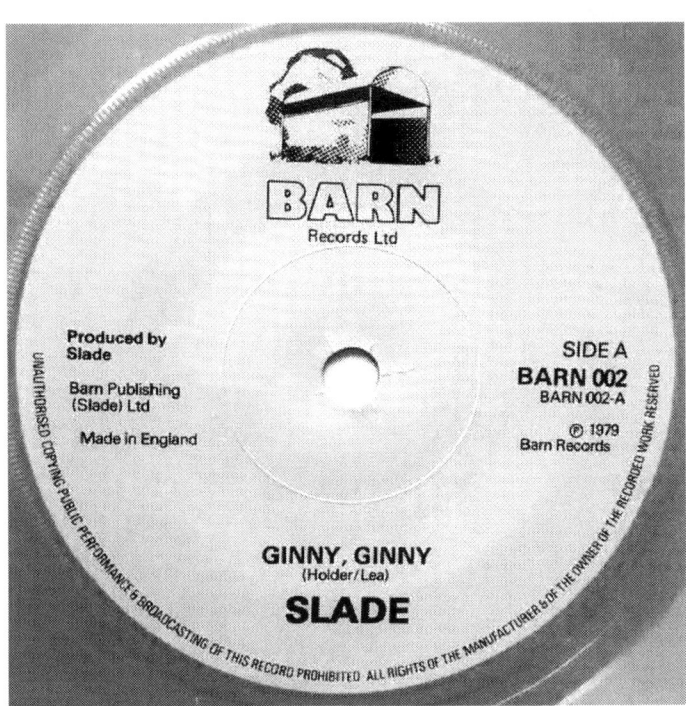

SLADE 'Ginny, Ginny' (Barn)
Another stab at stardom from the once superb Slade. A lot better than previous comeback attempts but still not quite strong enough to compete with other chart contenders I fear. Hope I'm wrong 'cos I used to love them. Is it all over now? The single is pressed on yuk yellow vinyl. Suppose it may help sell a few more copies.

SLADE: 'Ginny Ginny' (Barn). The climb back isn't going to be easy for Slade, but this might be a foothold on the bottom of the charts for them. Not the Big One though, even is Nod has got a great voice.

Saturday 26th - Manchester Polytech. Cavendish House, Cavendish St.

MANCHESTER POLYTECHNIC STUDENTS UNION

PRESENTS

SATURDAY 26TH MAY

MAY BALL

S L A D E
+ SUPPORT

2.00 TICKET ONLY

8.00PM

000115

CAV HSE
ALL SAINTS

Sunday 27th:
Don's diary said that Noddy Holder had rang him to say that they had got into the Sunday papers because they had cancelled a Student gig at a university because their drinks 'rider' had not been met.

THIRSTY SLADE ROCKS THE RAG BALL

By TONY ROBINSON

STUDENTS holding a charity dance are angry with top pop group, Slade.

Just nine days ago, the rock band cancelled a booking to appear at last night's Bedfordshire Students' Rag Week Ball.

"We have lost £150 because of this," said rag ball organiser Steve Skelton.

"We were hoping to raise £1,000 for five charities. Now we'll be lucky to break even."

Slade were to get £1,250 for an hour's performance.

But Steve, 21, revealed that the group expected more than cash.

He said: "Their drink requirements were massive. They wanted £50 worth of alcohol — bottles of whisky and vodka, the works! And they wanted food."

Mr. Mike Hales, boss of Slade's record company, Barn Records, said: "The students should not have gone ahead with preparations for the concert before confirmation of the booking.

"Slade have been delayed in the recording studio.

"As for the drink, the £50 figure seems high. I think it was nearer £25.

"It's a standard requirement in any artist's contract."

The rag ball went ahead with two other groups.

SUNDAY MIRROR, May 20, 1979

Tuesday 29th
Oscars Club,
Hanover Street, Liverpool

Thursday 31st
Allied Breweries Club.
Station St,
Burton-On-Trent.

JUNE 1979
Friday 1st
Grand Pavilion.
Queen St,
Withernsea.
Support: Nick Van Eede

Posters also exist which show Eazie as being the support group at this show.

GRAND PAVILION, WITHERNSEA
FRIDAY, 1ˢᵗ JUNE, 1979

SLADE

WITH SUPPORTING ARTISTE

NICK VAN EDE

AND THE

BIG M RECORD ROAD SHOW

DANCING 8-30 P.M. TO 1-00 A.M.

ADMISSION BY TICKET	AT THE DOOR
£2-00	£2-50

NO ADMISSION AFTER 11-00 P.M.
UNDER 16's NOT ADMITTED

Tickets available from :— Music Shop, Yates Newsagency, Chocolate Box

Saturday 2nd - Pavilion. West Runton
Support: Nick Van Eede

Monday 4th - Fiesta Club. Norton Road, Norton, Stockton on Tees

Thursday 7th – Don Powell is interviewed:

Q: How has he recording been for the new album?
A: Great. We're producing ourselves now and we've just been in the studios. There are quite a few songs done. I think we've got about 17 tracks actually recorded. Not all of them are completed, but things are going well.

Q: Are any of those tracks potential singles?

A: Well, what we are going to do is finish them all off first and then have a listen to them one by one and choose one. If, in the past, we'd put about three tracks down and then chosen a single out of those three, sometimes later we would record another batch of songs and then found that we'd have been more pleased with others in that batch.

Q: Were you pleased with the way that Ginny Ginny turned out, then?

A: Oh yeah! It didn't sell enough to get into the charts, but we were pleased with it.

Q: Once again the B-side Dizzy mama was great. Was it intentional that it should be a good B-side?

A: Not really. It's probably due to the fact that the recordings in general are getting better. A lot of acts record an A-side and then think 'Stick anything on the B-side.' But we've never thought like that. We've tried to put a track equal to the A-side on the B-side.

Q: With the production, is it the group as a whole that produce, or is it any particular member, in general?

A: Yes, we produce all the material ourselves. We each take a share in doing different things.

Q: What about Chas? Does he guide you at all?

A: Well, during office hours, he pops in and has a listen and makes a comment, or he'll advise us about something.

Q: Are there any plan to do a tour at the moment?

A: I think that there are some dates being lined up for September. I'm not sure that anything has been confirmed, but what I've heard is that there should be dates in September.

Q: You are still keen on doing all these concerts then?

A: Yes! That's our biggest sort of thrill – going on stage and playing, no matter what country it's in.

Q: Why haven't you done any dates in the South, or in Scotland on the last couple of tours?

A: I don't really know, because I never really think about it 'til somebody like yourself mentions it. It's not intentional. I suppose it's just the availability of halls and things like that.

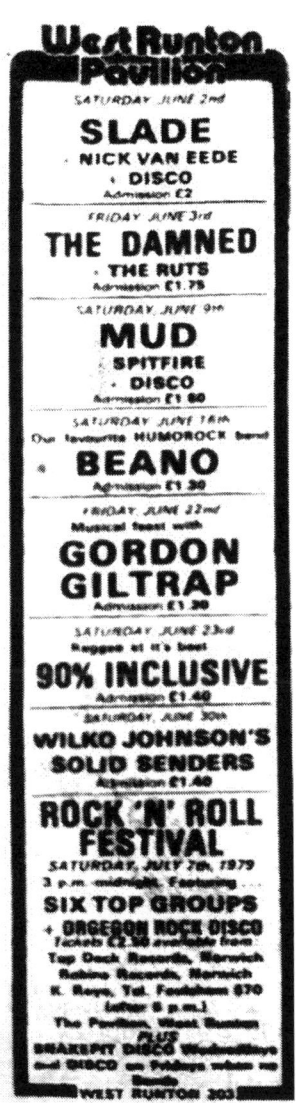

Q: *Have you made any new plans to go abroad?*

A: *Not really. Something may come up, but we've got the British dates first. They are sort of planned. Then maybe some plans will come up for Europe.*

Q: *Do you ever think about going back to America now?*

A: *We spent two years over there, actually based in the States, and that meant leaving Britain and the rest of Europe out.... Which is a long time to not actually work in either place, so we've decided to concentrate more on Britain and Europe now.*

Q: *Did you ever get really big in any particular areas over there?*

A: *Certain places were great for us.... Areas like St. Louis ad down in the Mid-West and the South.*

Q: *Did you just live in hotels when you were over there?*

A: *You travel every day. You arrive in one city, check in at the hotel, do the concert, check out the next morning, and then fly on somewhere else.*

Q: *You had no settled base then?*

A: *We actually lived in New York and we'd try to get back there as much as possible, but the States are so big that you cannot get back home every night like you can in England.*

Q: *On your last American tour in '75 were you headlining?*
A: *It all depends on what state we were in, whether we were strong enough to headline or not.*

Q: *Have you ever thought of doing any large festival-type concerts, like you did in America, over here, like Reading or Knebworth?*
A: *I wouldn't have minded doing something like that, but not this year. It's a bit late now. I think some of the festivals have finished now. There may be a few more to be done, but probably they have their line-ups already fixed.*

Q: *Apart from concerts, you haven't got any TV work lined up, have you?*

A: It all depends on the singles, really... whether they can get any TV promotion. The last thing I heard was the offices were trying to get Flame on television, but I don't know what you have to go through to achieve that kind of thing.

Q: Have you personally ever considered moving back to Wolverhampton?

A: A couple of times I have, but I think that I would miss not being able to get to concerts quickly. There's not many concerts in Wolves, or around that sort of area. There's a lot more going on in London.

Q: How do you like living in London now?

A: It's OK. At first I couldn't stand the place, but it's just a matter of adapting really. You learn to make friends, you get places to go...

Don's diary: "I left for Portsmouth to get the ferry to Guernsey. Checked in the hotel to find, I'd left my diary on the ferry."

Friday 8th
Sir John Loveridge Hall. Beau Lejour Leisure Centre, Guernsey
Support: Streetcar

Slade – while still languishing in their chart doldrums – actually drew a bigger crowd than Status Quo.

Don's diary: *"Got up at 11:00 am. Made tea - and my diary had been delivered to the hotel from the ferry company!! I played tapes in my room before having tea with Willi, Charlie (sound guy) Jude & Harry (lighting guys). Jude had broken a tooth falling off a ladder setting the lights up! Great gig, drank in the hotel after."*

Super Slade on make or break visit

SUPER Slade showed Guernsey fans last night that they have lost none of their old magic.

The Wolverhampton rock band delivered close on an hour and a half of high energy music to their noisily enthusiastic audience.

But the whole evening was touch and go. Yesterday's poor weather left organisers Ace Promotions guessing until 9 p.m. before the fourth member of the band finally arrived in the island.

He was lead singer Noddy Holder, whose day started at 5 a.m. when he left Birmingham for Heathrow. His flight was diverted to Jersey and, as the fog closed in again in the early evening, he was forced to catch the ferry to Guernsey.

The fans—there were an estimated 1,400—knew nothing of this. Neither did Slade's stunning performance give any hint of the difficulties Noddy, and the other members, had in getting here.

Tidal waves of sound filled Beau Sejour's Sir John Loveridge Hall as the band crashed into number after number to fulfil its opening promise: "We're going to have a rock and roll evening."

Guitarist Dave Hill and bassist Jimmy Lea whirled around the specially-erected stage with Noddy Holder while drummer Don Powell remained virtually hidden behind his kit and, at times, thick multi-coloured smoke.

There is a serious side to Slade's visit, however. Ace Promotions need at least 2,000 people at tonight's concert to have any chance of attracting further top class bands to Guernsey.

Organiser Phil Davies said last night that Slade's appearance is virtually a make or break visit. Unless he gets the 2,000 attendance other bands in the same class won't be interested in coming.

He is going to London next week to discuss further bookings and, subject to tonight's turn-out, hopes to bring the next band across within six to eight weeks.

Mr Davies would not say which group he has in mind other than commenting that it is of the same standing as Thin Lizzy or Leo Sayer.

Credit was also due to local band Streetcar, which had the unenviable task of warming up 1,400 people all waiting for Slade.

Police and St John Ambulance personnel were able to enter into the spirit of the concert—which many said more than equalled that given by Status Quo—because it was so trouble-free. "Very quiet," they commented!

Saturday 9th
Sir John Loveridge Hall. Beau Lejour Leisure Centre, Guernsey
Support: Streetcar

Don's diary said that they enjoyed the second show.

ACE PROMOTIONS
presents

& SUPPORT BAND
'STREETCAR'

In Concert at
Beau Sejour Leisure Centre

**8 p.m. to midnight
8th & 9th JUNE, 1979**

TICKETS £2.75

AVAILABLE FROM BEAU SEJOUR
BOOKING OFFICE OR RING
ACE PROMOTIONS 65310

LICENSED BAR & REFRESHMENTS

Monday 11th
Don's diary reported that he spent the evening with Andy Mackay of Roxy music and his partner.

Monday 18th: Portland Recording Studio

19th - Portland Recording Studio.

20th – Portland Recording Studio.

21st – Portland Recording Studio.

22nd – Portland Recording Studio.

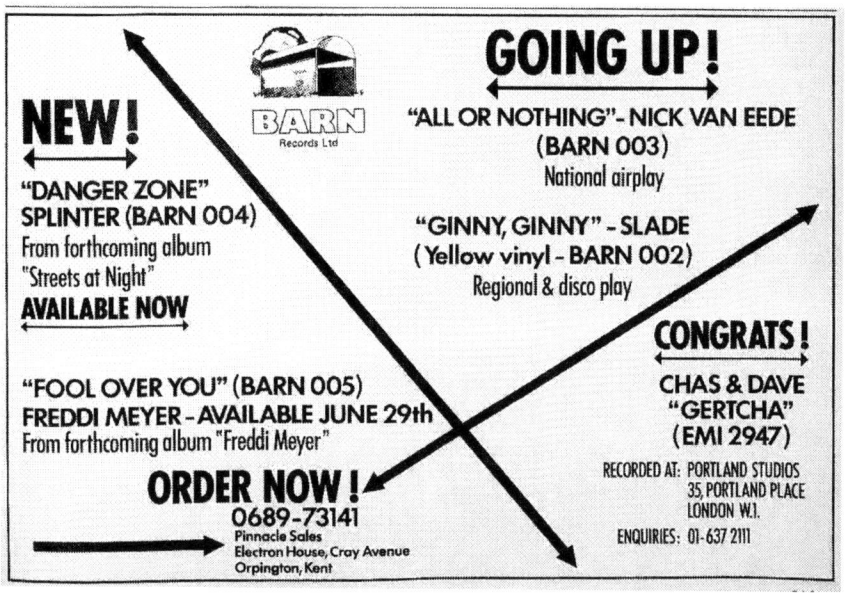

JULY 1979
2nd: Don Powell, Noddy Holder and Keith Atham travelled to Wales to attend for the court case against the nightclub bouncer who assaulted Noddy Holder, breaking his nose the previous year

Thursday 5th : *The verdict of the court case against the club bouncer who assaulted Noddy Holder was heard in Cardiff.*

Desmond Brothers was sentenced to a three month jail term for the assault.

The result was all over the national press.

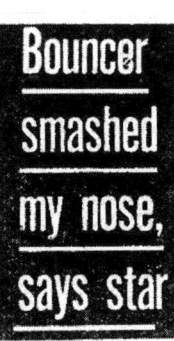

Bouncer smashed my nose, says star

SINGER Noddy Holder of the rock group Slade told a court yesterday how he ended up with a broken nose in a pop concert punch-up.

And he claimed that a bouncer hired to protect the group — threw the punch that did the damage.

Holder, 29, told Cardiff Crown Court that he halted the concert before 500 fans in Porthcawl, Glamorgan as bouncers became "very aggressive," and were "pushing people around."

Grabbed

He told one bouncer: "You must be a big boy picking on people half your size." And the bouncer replied: "I'll see you later on."

Holder said that later the same bouncer grabbed him outside his dressing room and punched him in the face.

Bouncer Desmond Brothers, 29, of Pyle, Glamorgan, denies causing grievous bodily harm to Holder.

Jail for breaking Noddy's nose

A nightclub bouncer who assaulted ,Noddy Holder lead singer with the pop group Slade, breaking his nose, was jailed for three months yesterday. Desmond Brothers, 29, a former trainee policeman, of Pyle Inn Way, Pyle, near Bridgend, Glamorgan, attacked Holder at the end of the group's performance at a South Wales nightclub.

Holder, who admitted that it had been a riotous evening' with fans jumping on tables and shouting, told Cardiff Crown Court that he interrupted the group's performance when he became concerned at the way bouncers were pushing the audience around.

He pointed to Brothers and warned over the microphone : 'You must be a big guy picking on people half your size.'

After the performance, as the group were returning to their dressing room at the Stoneleigh Club, Porthcawl, Glamorgan. Brothers grabbed Holder around the neck and said: 'I am the fellow you were talking to.' He then punched Holder in the face, breaking his nose.

The 29-year-old pop singer, real name Neville John Holder, of Chelsea Embankment, London, crashed over backwards, his face covered in blood. He was later taken to hospital for treatment to a broken nose.

Passing sentence. Judge Michael Gibbon told Brothers: 'You are a man with a violent temper. I accept there was some provocation, cut not of the type that other people would react to with violence.

The court was told that Brothers had previously been sentenced to 12 months imprisonment for wounding while working as a bouncer at another South Wales nightclub.

CUM ON FEEL THE NOZE

BOUNCER Desmond Brothers was sentenced to three months imprisonment at Cardiff Crown Court for causing grievous bodily harm to Slade singer Noddy Holder after a gig at Porthcawl.

Brothers broke Holder's nose with a punch after Holder had accused him of being too rough with fans while the band were playing on stage. Holder shouted out to him: "You must be a big boy picking on people half your size." After the gig Brothers followed Holder to the dressing room and assaulted him.

Guitarist Jim Lea told the court that the bouncers were "aggressive and violent and were thumping some of the kids."

After Brothers, aged 29 from Pyle near Bridgend, was found guilty of the assault it was revealed in court that he had a similar conviction already and was a former policeman.

Bouncer found guilty of Slade assault

Noddy Holder practicing karate chops. Pic: Joe Stevens.

WELSH BOUNCER Desmond Brothers was jailed last week for three months after being found guilty of inflicting grievious bodily harm on Slade's Noddy Holder.

Cardiff Crown Court heard how Brothers attacked Holder back stage at Stoneleigh Club in Porthcawl, South Wales, last August following a gig at which Holder stopped the music after seeing bouncers laying into fans at the front of the stage.

"They were punching them in the face," he told Thrills. "Okay, the kids were getting up and dancing but there was no call for punching them. We're used to having that reaction every night so we are used to controlling the crowd."

One bouncer, Desmond Brothers, was being particularly violent so Holder shouted through the mike: "You must be a big boy picking on people half your size." Brothers said he'd see Holder later but Slade resumed their set and Holder thought no more of the incident.

They had completed their set when Brothers came backstage and said: "I'm the fellow you were talking to." Seconds later he punched Holder, who still had his guitar strapped round his neck, knocking him to the floor.

Holder was taken to hospital and found to be suffering from a broken nose.

In his defence Brothers said that Holder had slapped him in the face and that one of the group's roadies had punched him in the ribs. He also said that Holder had humiliated him in front of the audience.

After the jury had reached their verdict Brothers, a former police cadet asked for one previous conviction for malicious wounding to be taken into account.

Holder told Thrills: "I think there's a minority of bouncers who are just out for a punch up and when they've had a couple of drinks they're looking for the first opportunity to bop somebody.

"In a way the club is as guilty as the bouncer is. They should know what sort of blokes they're employing and how they handle the job. About 80 per cent of bouncers can handle the audience how they should be handled.

"The bouncers who know their job can go in, break up a fight, take the offending guys out and nobody will realise what has happened. These bouncers do a good job.

"I think innocent kids that are hurt by bouncers should prosecute. That way bouncers might think twice before attacking an innocent party."

STEVE CLARKE

THRILLS

Bouncer jailed for attack on Noddy

A BAD-TEMPERED night club bouncer was jailed for three months yesterday for punching pop star Noddy Holder.

Desmond Brothers, 29, attacked Holder, lead singer with Slade, after the group's performance at Stoneleigh club in Porthcawl, South Wales.

Brothers, a former trainee policeman, of Pyle Inn Way, Pyle, near Bridgend, pleaded not guilty at Cardiff Crown Court to assault.

He claimed the pop star insulted him then attacked him. Holder, 29, was taken to hospital with a broken nose.

Judge Michael Gibbon told Brothers, who had a previous conviction for malicious wounding: "You are a man with a violent temper."

SMASH HIT FOR NODDY

Bouncer broke my nose claims Noddy

EXPRESS REPORTER

A RAVE-UP at a pop concert ended with singer Noddy Holder of "Slade" nursing a broken nose, a court heard yesterday. It was all due to club bouncers being too aggressive with fans, the 29-year-old pop star claimed.

ROCK star Noddy Holder, lead singer with Slade, ended up with a broken nose after a riotous concert.

And the man who broke it was a bouncer, a court heard.

Holder, 29, said he protested to concert steward Desmond Brothers over his "very aggressive" behaviour.

Later, he said, Brothers grabbed him and punched him in the face.

"I fell to the floor covered in blood," Holder told Cardiff Crown Court.

Brothers, 29, of Pyle near Bridgend denies the assault. The case continues.

He told Cardiff Crown Court that the stewards were creating a bad atmosphere by pushing people around.

He said to one of them over a microphone: "You must be a big boy taking on people half your size."

It was alleged the man replied: "Call me what you like—I'll see you later."

Holder described his group's performance as "very riotous."

Fell

When the show at the Stoneleigh Club, Porthcawl, Glamorgan, was over, Holder said a man approached him backstage, put his arm around his shoulder and said: "I'm the big boy who talked to you."

When Holder replied: "Yeah," the man punched him on the nose.

Said Holder: "I fell to the floor. All I can remember is that he was a dark, broad-shouldered fellow."

Holder, of Chelsea Embankment, London, was giving evidence against club steward Desmond Brothers, who is charged with inflicting grievous bodily harm on him.

Brothers, aged 29, of Pyle, Glamorgan, denies the charge.

The hearing continues.

NODDY HOLDER
Broken nose
DAILY EXPRESS Tuesday July 3 1979

Wednesday 11th
Portland Recording Studio, putting tambourine and tom-tom overdubs on 'Hold On To Your Hats'.

Friday 13th
Portland Recording Studio - mixing.

AUGUST 1979

15th - Don recording at EMI studios with Steve McNerney and Charlie McCracken.

SEPTEMBER 1979

11th - Don at EMI studios with Steve and Ian - sax player with Burlesque.

30th - Slade rehearsals

OCTOBER 1979

1st - Slade rehearsals.
The album Return To Base was released on Barn NARB003.

Coming on a very basic red plain cover, the album was a very mixed bag of styles and moods.

Wheels Ain't Coming Down was a straight chugging rocker, which dealt with the subject matter of a nightmare plane ride and the relief when the wheels were coming down after all.

Hold On To Your Hats was Slade's attempt at a clattering, noisy disco track. It features very strong riffs throughout on guitars and bass and this is probably what Noddy Holder always used to talk about when he talked about all three of them powering through a song playing the same thing.

Chakeeta was a funky little track, quite unlike Slade in many ways, though the choruses give away who's playing.

Don't Waste Your Time (Back Seat Star) is almost a country and western song. Totally different for Slade? Listen to a couple of the tracks on the Nobody's Fools album, and it's not a great leap to get to this.

Sign Of The Times is a weary recording. The band sound a bit tired and unenthusiastic. It's just too slow and doesn't really take off, even on the choruses. The word RADIO is used a lot, as that was a thing at the time, a good ploy to get radio plays. It would be lifted for a single and would die an ignoble death.

I'm A Rocker was a Chuck Berry song that Noddy Holder brought forward for the group to do. It is arranged entirely differently to the original, which meanders along, not going anywhere. Slade's version is more powerful straight forward and focussed and a lot faster. A good choice for them to do and they really sound like they are having fun recording it. This would get into the live show for a while, along with a cover of Boney Maronie.

Nuts Bolts And Screws is an excellent rocker with plain silly lyrics.

My Baby's Got It sees Slade returning to writing one of those good old rock and roll songs. It's rather derivative of everything which went before in the 1950's which is what makes it so great. Nearly all of the greatest 1950's rock and roll hits were sort of clones of each other, so the group can be completely forgiven. It would be used for a B-side.

I'm Mad was a song that Jim Lea envisioned as being in the style of a more psychedelic Beatles track. He had asked Don Powell to listen to the drums on Strawberry fields Forever before the recording, but the track did end up sounding like Slade in the end. The Beatles influence can't be denied and this catchy song could have been a single rather than Sign Of The Times. But it wasn't... sadly. It too would later be excised for use as a B-side.

Lemme Love Into Ya is a slow, moody track that picks up pace and is startlingly effective. It made it into the stage act and it made a point of featuring Dave Hill on rather dramatic lead guitar. Jim Lea would later re-record the track under the name Poland with a vocoder voice and different lyrics and it was also released a number of times as an instrumental version.

Ginny Ginny was a truly great and very catchy pop track that worked well onstage, where it had a degree of power that the studio recording somehow lacked. This would be lifted as a single. It is a shame that a decent live recording of this song has not surfaced officially.

Slade also recorded a cover of Andy Miller's song, Another Win, under duress, which didn't make the album and is unlikely to be released. Making them break off from what they were doing to take on this song badly soured their relationship with Chas Chandler.

The album cover was just disappointing and some fans say that Slade didn't even want their faces on the front of an album cover at this point.

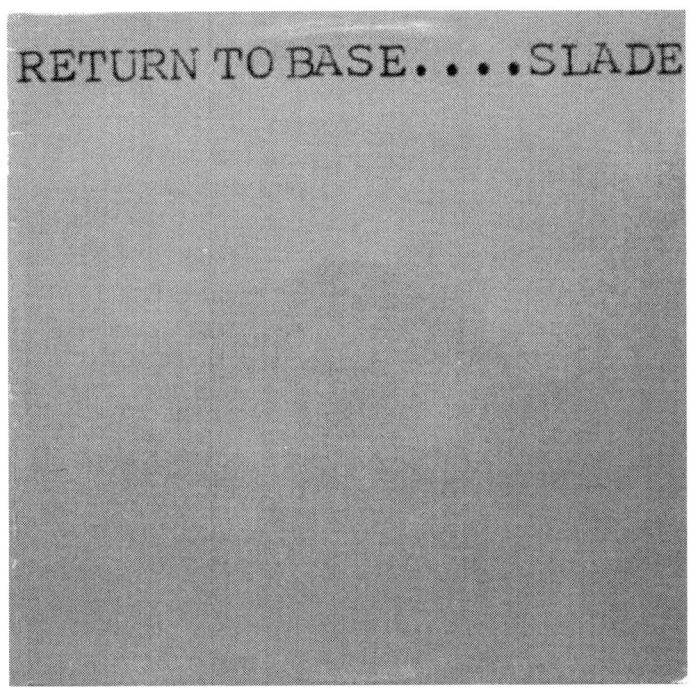

The album did well in Belgium, reaching number one on one of their charts, but sadly didn't do very well at all in the UK. It is now one of their rarer albums. The press gleefully took the opportunity to sharpen their knives.

SLADE
Return To Base *(Barn)*
SLADE always were a poor man's hard rock band, appealing to the worst boys-night-out instincts. In the days when bad glam rock was the British norm this sort of muck might have fitted the bill a treat, but in 1979 who wants to hear a bunch of pathetic old has-been Flash Harrys reiterating the limitations of their puerile sordid imaginations? Haven't these people heard of social security?

SLADE 'Return To Base' (BARN NARB 003).

ASSUMING THAT the title 'Return To Base' should be taken to mean that the group are trying to revisit the territorial war grounds of their golden years in the singles charts I reckon they're in for a shock.

At one time everyone loved Slade. Noddy Holder's John Lennon impersonation taken to an extreme coupled with those wonnerful rockin melodies, and one of the best Christmas songs of all time, ensured them a permanent holding in the top ten. However, as everyone knows the Slades went off on the Queen Mary one day when they should have stayed up in Birmingham and I very much doubt if anyone cares if they came back or not. I accept that Slade are not the most intelligent of men (witness the feature 'Slade In Flame') but then that's not what I demand from my pop stars, but I do expect a little more than references to Big Brother, Stereo, Radio etc in the otherwise catchy 'Sign Of The Times' and the reflection of 'Born To Run' in the opener 'Wheels Ain't Coming Down'.

Noddy's vocal prowess certainly hasn't dimmed on 'I'm A Rocker' and on 'Nuts, Bolts And Screws' and 'My Baby's Got It' Slade start to rock but there's nothing here to distinguish them from any other rockin' combo.

'I'm Mad' is the nearest thing here to a hit single with its jumpalong beat and pure sixties chord changes. The production is by the band and Andy Miller which really is excellent, especially the little tricks like the tremaloed backward guitar intro on 'Lemme Love Into Ya' and the very ambient sound throughout. I wasn't expecting another 'Cum On Feel The Noize' or 'My Friend Stan' but just something a little more inspired. From a new band this would be a fairly good debut. From Slade I want more. + + + **JAMES PARADE**

Slade return to basics

SLADE haven't had a big hit for some time now, but it would be silly to write them off just yet, to judge by their new album, Return To Base.

Still one of the most entertaining live groups around, they have too much talent not to get another hit, but I'm not sure if they'll hit the mark with their new single. They've revived the Hokey Cokey, no less.

It's their contender for the Christmas charts, and it will certainly get a few parties going if it's put on the turntable.

Slade's version is a hard-rocking, full of fun song which combines their musical toughness and ability to create a good time atmosphere to perfection.

The song really suits Slade's style, but whether or not it will be a hit is anyone's guess.

I don't know whether Return To Base refers to their music, but there is definitely a Sixties feel to some of the songs, though others are vintage Slade.

Most striking thing about the album is its variety, for Slade have loosened up a bit for this one and included much more variety of mood. It certainly pays off.

As usual they start off with force, singing a song which went down well everywhere on their last tour. It's called Wheels Ain't Coming Down, a power-packed churning song with a catchy hook line.

After that, however, come all sorts of songs from frantic ravers to more gentle songs. One, which sounds similar to Bob Dylan's early tracks with The Band, especially the organ sound, really takes the ear — it's called Don't Waste Your Time.

Another striking factor is the guitar playing of Dave Hill, who has really been allowed to branch out on this disc.

In all, it's an album which will please Slade's still huge army of fans, both for its fidelity to the Slade sound and for its inventiveness and freshness.

John Ogden

SLADE
'Return To Base'
(BARN NARB003)*

SLADE STARTED life in the sixties as a Wolverhampton club band called the In-betweens who changed their name to Ambrose Slade, eventually dropping the Ambrose at the suggestion of erstwhile Animal Chas Chandler. As Slade they came to the media's attention because of their skinhead image (later played down with bullshit about their cropped barnets stemming from working abroad) which was widely reported around the time of their first hit single, a raucous revamp of Bobby Marchan's 'Get Down And Get With It'.

Thenceforth they established themselves as possibly the biggest of the glitter generation teen bands banging home an unbroken succession of hits including six number ones, capturing the imagination and support of millions of kids (including me) with their illiterate brand of glitter-stomp ie, 'Gudbye T' Jane', 'Mama Weer All Crazee Now', and the definitive 'Cum On Feel The Noize', changing direction in later life with the likes of 'My Friend Stan' and the more bailady 'Far Far Away' and 'Everyday', before fading out of the public eye 'till their disappointing 're-incarnation' tour last year.

Like most people I take the purist view that rock 'n' roll heroes should die, or at least retire gracefully, before the rot sets in (nothing's quite so disgusting as seeing latter day teen heroes squirming on good ol' family TV) and though recording the 'Hokey Cokey' is tantamount to public suicide Slade have managed to pull a fair to impressive performance out of the bag with this one.

Sure to new wave lugs it sound well dated but 'Base' still rocks like a good 'un utilising standard rock 'n' roll/hard rock foundations for commendable displays of tightness and old-time rock bite. And I'm sure it ain't just nostalgia bringing me to the conclusion that Noddy's got one of the all time classic rock voices — as he belts thru' ten steamy originals and one Chuck Berry (who else?) cover.

Slade may have stood still but their own brand of rock-shout clout still sounds good to these biased ears.

GARRY BUSHELL

Tuesday 2nd – Wales Polytechnic, Main Hall, Treforest, Wales

POLYTECHNIC OF WALES
STUDENTS UNION

POLY ENTS

proudly presents for the

COMING-UP BALL

SLADE

plus SUPPORT and DISCO

Tuesday, 2nd October
Main Hall, Treforest at 8 p.m.

TICKETS

£1.50 (in advance); £1.75 (on door)
(all tickets include V.A.T.)

Bar till midnight

Wednesday 3rd -. University Student Union, Park Place, Cardiff, Wales
Support: Saxon

Thursday 4th - Civic Hall. North Street, Wolverhampton
Support: Def Leppard.

A highlight of the show was a new and very different version of their old hit Look Wot You Dun, which they played at this one show, after jamming it out at a recent rehearsal. It is uncertain whether they actually played it again later on in the tour.

Back home in triumph for powerhouse Slade

Noddy Holder and Dave Hill, playing for all they were worth, when glimpsed through the waving arms and dry ice at The Civic Hall, Wolverhampton, put me more in mind of Motorhead, rather than the group that held sway over the pop charts in Britain in the early to middle Seventies.

Noddy's gritty vocals, Dave Hill's powerful guitar work, Jimmy Lea's intense bass and violin playing, with Don Powell's thunderous support showed what a powerhouse Slade have become.

The audience had been singing and shouting for them from the moment that the support band left the stage. The atmosphere was like a fooball match with singing and chanting people swaying to and fro.

It did not take long for the local heroes to win over the audience with oldies such at "Take Me Back 'ome"; "Gudbuy t'Jane"; and newies like "The Wheels Ain't Comin' Down", which proved that the quality of their writing is as good as it ever was.

After only 40 minutes they "finished" with "Get Down and Get With It" — but there was still a lot to come.

They returned triumphantly with a further set of oldies, and by this time the audience was ecstatic.

The band stayed on stage for nearly as long again, and the sight of toilet rolls being shot at the audience from the stage, balloons falling from the roof, and Noddy Holder dressed as Santa Claus while singing Merry Christmas Everybody took the chill away from a cold winter night and proved conclusively what great showmen Slade are.

Pictured are members of Slade and three fans before the concert, from left, Alison Orton, aged 16, from Wombourne, Dave Hill, Dawn Wilson, aged 16, from Wombourne, Jimmy Lea, Don Powell, Liz Lister, aged 15, from Sedgley, and Noddy Holder.

J.J.O.

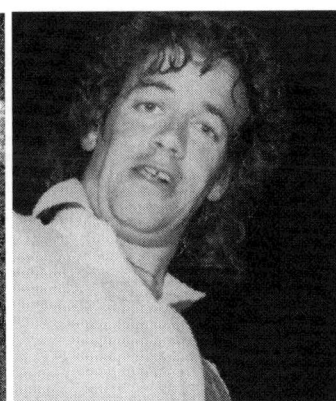

Friday 5th - University .Southampton

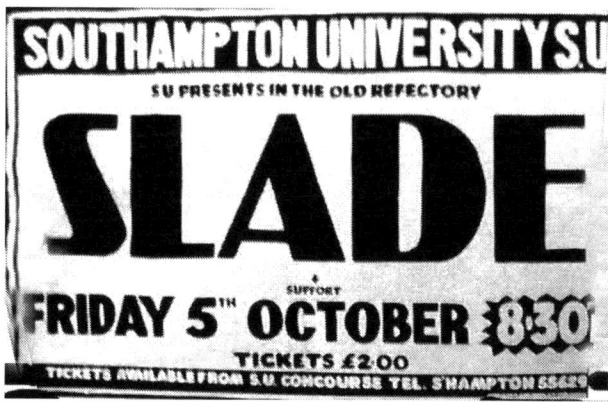

Saturday 6th - East Anglia University, Norwich

Don's diary said that Len Tuckey came to the show with Suzi Quatro.

Monday 8th - Hamilton Club. Henry Street, Birkenhead
Support Nick Van Eede.

Tuesday 9th - Tiffany's Nightclub. St Stephens St, Edinburgh.

Don's diary stated that the group drove home to Wolverhampton after the show and that he got to bed at 6.30am.

Thursday 11th - Baileys Nightclub, Leicester.

Friday 12th - City University, London.

Saturday 13th - University – Nottingham.
Support: Def Leppard.

NOTTINGHAM UNIV. S.U. CONCERTS. OCTOBER 79

SIOUXSIE AND THE BANSHEES — MON 1
The most powerful, disturbing Band in the World. The Tour goes ahead with Budgie (Slits) on drums and Robert Smith (Cure) on guitar. Support are The Cure.

THE RUTS — WED 3
If "In a Rut" was a great debut single the follow-ups "Babylon's Burning" and the current hit "Something that I said" show the tremendous depth of talent in this Band. They are going to be enormous in the 80's so catch them while you can.

WEEK ONE PARTY — SAT 6
The Photos - supporting on the Squeeze Tour. The Lambrettas - best Brighton Rock I've sampled. Thunderbirds - stole the show at Hyson Green Festival + Discos, Films, Local Bands, Late Bar.

MADNESS + MERTON PARKAS — WED 10
At the forefront of the Ska and Mod revivals are these two Bands. But the success of both lies in the fact that they renew rather than revive - they use the musical lessons of the past 15 years to take the "Spirit of '64" into the 80's. Beware of cheap imitations.

SLADE + DEF LEPPARD — SAT 13
Amazing live, as anyone who saw them last year will testify. Cum on feel the noyze.
Blew Sammy Hagar off-stage prompting Phonogram to snap them up for one of the biggest advances ever made to a Band. Living proof that Heavy Metal is not dead.

Monday 15th - Bunnies Club. Grant St, Cleethorpes.

Tuesday 16th - Bunnies Club, Grant St, Cleethorpes.

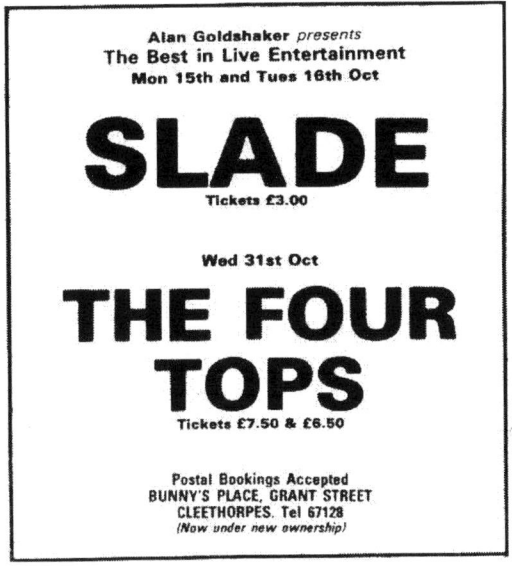

Thursday 18th - Sandman Club. Princess Margaret Way, Port Talbot

Friday 19th - Barbarellas Club. Cumberland Street, Birmingham

Saturday 20th - Music Machine. High Street, Camden, London
Support: En Route

SLADE
Music Machine, London

SLADE WERE left stranded when the tide of the new wave ran through the music business.

The fact that Slade made their reputation as one of the best nights out in the country has been obscured by the glitter of yesteryear.

This conditioning has detracted from the fact that they are impeccable musicians. Sure, Dave Hill still wiggles his bum while teetering dangerously on his high heels, but his guitar playing is always fresh, assured and entertaining — even without the lunatic visuals.

Jimmy Lea provides a standard of bass guitar virtuosity that merges perfectly with the relentless pounding of Don Powell's drums.

Noddy Holder still displays that legendary fog horn voice, that's hard, gritty and raspy, a classic rock 'n' roll blunt instrument.

The oldies like 'Take Me Back Home', 'Look What You've Done', 'Gud Bye T'Jane' 'Mamma We're All Crazy Now' all sounded even fresher than my memory lead me to expect. The tracks they played from their new album 'Returning To Base' sounded equally interesting.

Slade are as good a slice of text book loud, raucous, rowdy, rock 'n' roll spirit as you are likely to see.

It's time for a revaluation of Slade and it might as well start with you. I advise you to come and feel the noise soon. MIKE GARDNER

RETURN OF SLADE

SLADE are back on the road. The group will commence a series of dates on October 3 at Cardiff University to coincide with a new album released on Barn Records.

Full tour dates available: Civic Hall, Wolverhampton (4); Southampton University (5); Norwich University, East Anglia (6); Hamilton Club, Birkenhead (8); Tiffany's, Edinburgh (9); Bailey's, Leicestershire (11); City University, London (12); Nottingham University (13); Bunnies, Cleethorpes (15, 16); Barbarellas, Birmingham (19); Civic Hall, Dunstable (21); Top Rank, Sheffield (22).

Slade's new album, 'Return To The Base' is planned for release at the end of the month and 'Sign Of The Times' is a new 45 heralding the album released this week on Barn.

Slade's Dave Hill

Sunday 21st - Queensway Hall. Court Drive, Dunstable.

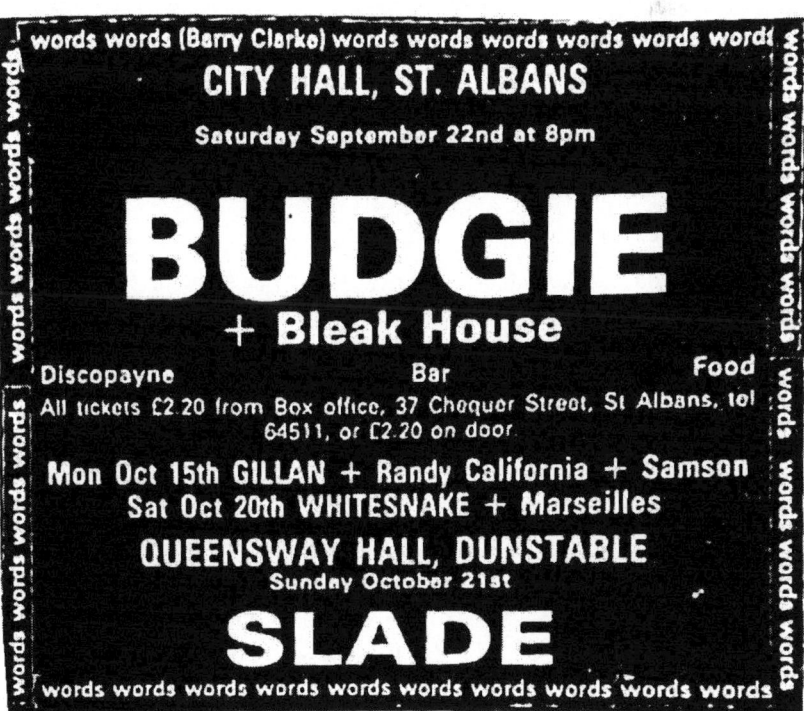

Monday 22nd - Top Rank – Sheffield.

Dave Hill was interviewed before this show for the fan newsletter.

Q: Dave, you say that the new album Return To Base will be out soon. Do you have any definite release date?

A: Not yet. It should be out before Christmas though. We thought we would release the single first though, and see what happens with that.

Q: How long in all did the album take to record?

A: It must have taken six weeks, on and off.

Q: Did any one member do the bulk of the work on the production side?

A: No, we each took it in turns to produce certain parts ourselves, which makes it the first album we have solely produced ourselves.

Q: The title Return To Base.... How did that come about?

A: Well, we had a whole list of suggestions for the title, and Return To Base is the one we eventually decided upon. Return To Base is from one of the lines of Sign Of The Times.

Q: Onto the cover. Has it been designed yet?

A: It's still being done, but I understand that it is going to have a photo of a tickertape message on the front, saying 'Return To Base' in computer-type lettering. But it should be a very basic cover, so that it ties in with the 'basic' reference in the title.

I'm very satisfied with it. It's got a mixture of different types of songs on it – all of which adds up to it being a very good album.

Q: What's your own favourite track on the record, then?

A: My favourites are the rock'n'roll one, I'm A Rocker and the instrumental one, Lemme love Into ya... probably because of the way that they come over on stage more than anything else.

Q: Onto the new stage act, how did the new version of Look Wot You Dun get back into the act, as you haven't played it live since 1973?

A: What happened was that we were doing a session and we suddenly started jamming it, and we took the song from there. We changed it from the original because we thought that it would have sounded a bit weak, so we made it a bit heavy for the current show.

We are planning to get some more tracks from the new album into the show, but we want to have the record released first, so at least the audience have an inkling as to what the songs are before we start playing all these new numbers onstage.

Q: Will you be adding some more songs, like Look Wot You Dun, to the set?

A: We've all agreed that there are no more oldies that we can re-do. We've got to go forward, not backward. For example, we've been doing a new song, The Wheels Ain't Comin' Down and that's been getting a fantastic reaction and nobody's heard it before. We've got to get new numbers like that into the show.

Q: Why haven't you been doing Sign Of The Times live?

A: The reason for that is that, at the moment, we feel the set is just about right. We have added two numbers that have worked very well and we are now hoping to get Sign Of The Times in, on the next stretch of dates. Also, at the moment, we've got one slow ballad in the act, and on this tour, we didn't want to have two.

Q: I've seen the new stage outfits of yours. Are they your own creations?

A: In a way I've designed them myself. I came along with the ideas and I took them to a lady called Jean Seal, who made the clothes for me. I've decided to return to wearing colourful stage outfits again, rather than maintaining the black and white look. Watching the music scene at the moment, what with the flashiness of the punks and also taking the theory that the whole music business revolves in a circle, I see it as inevitable that the glitter scene will come back again, and when it does, I'll be top of the pile!

Q: You've always liked wearing flash clothes, though, haven't you?

A: I like to get reactions by my clothes. I suppose it's a means of expressing myself. In many ways I felt like a punk in our early days, dressing weirdly, just for the hell of making people look! Even as a kid, I can remember wearing a cap and long cape and walking through Woolworths, so as to make everyone stop and stare!

Q: Will you be taking a trek abroad before the year's out?

A: We can always go abroad, bit while we've got the single out over here, and while we are trying to break back into the market again, we'd rather stay at home. We might do the occasional stint on the Continent, but not at the moment.

Q: This is the last night of the tour. How do you feel it has gone... well or badly?

A: It's gone well. Even you have seen that. Look at the Music Machine gig. There was a far bigger crowd there this year compared to last year's gig. It was packed out.

Q: One question that I've always wanted to ask you... What is your favourite record you have ever recorded?

A: My favourite of all time? We haven't recorded it yet.

Thursday 26th – Slade's Sign Of The Times / Not Tonight Josephine single was released on the Barn label.

The A-side was a rather slow and depressing track, which doesn't make for easy listening all these years later. The B-side wasn't slow and depressing. It was Slade on top form and should maybe have been the A-side. The single earned its low sales. It did not chart.

SLADE: "Sign Of The Times" (Barn 010). Poor old Slade. Banished by the fickle finger of public taste, they've been hovering in a sort of no-man's land for ages. This one won't recapture an audience, even though they're clearly aiming for the ELO sector. Echoed vocals, lots of bombast and the odd "electronic" gimmick do not a great single make. Only when Noddy Holder recaptures his perfect John Lennon imitation will they rise from the ashes

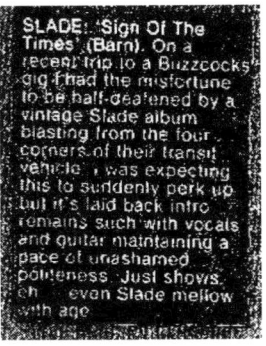

SLADE: Sign Of The Times (Barn). On a recent trip to a Buzzcocks' gig I had the misfortune to be half-deafened by a vintage Slade album blasting from the four corners of their transit vehicle. I was expecting this to suddenly perk up but it's laid back intro remains such with vocals and guitar maintaining a pace of unashamed politeness. Just shows, eh — even Slade mellow with age.

SLADE 'Sign Of The Times' Barn
I never was one for the rantings and ravings of Noddy Holder & Co. and this latest 45 doesn't do much to change my attitude.
Starting slowly and building up to the usual foot-stomping, heavy head banging climax; it's sure to go down well in the Northern clubs where the band have a fervent following.
I'd hate to think what the Southern crowds would say to this dated sound.
SUPERPOP RATING 2

SLADE: Sign Of The Times (Barn). Mind you, so's this. People are still asking whatever happened to Slade, and — judging by this bewildered Beatley ballad — not a lot has occurred since the last time the question was asked. The saga of Slade should stand as an Awful Warning to successful British bands who are determined to crack the States and keep playing the States until it happens. If it doesn't (as it didn't to Slade), you end up as much of a nonentity in your homeland as you are over there. *That's* what happened to Slade.

Saturday 27th October 1979 - University - Guildford, Surrey

Sunday 28th October 1979 - University – Bradford

Monday 29th October 1979 - Assembly Rooms – Derby

Tuesday 30th October 1979 - Music Machine - Camden, London

NOVEMBER 1979

6th – Portland Recording Studio, London.

The group recorded their rock version of the song Hokey Cokey. Don Powell and Jim Lea were not happy to be doing it. Dave just went with the majority. Noddy Holder seems to have been the driving force behind the decision to record the song.

Noddy Holder later explained in a video interview with Chris Selby and Ian Edmundson that Okey Cokey had been recorded at Polydor's request as an extra track for a seasonal EP, which would have been headed by Merry Xmas Everybody. They were too late getting into the studio, so the finished track missed the schedule for getting the Christmas EP pressed up, so Polydor had simply pressed up a supply of the regular single in readiness for Christmas. The previous year had seen a projected Hits EP with Merry Xmas everybody as the lead track, but it was shelved at the last minute.

Jim Lea has been quoted as saying he absolutely hated the very idea of recording the song and was told that if he didn't turn up in the studio, it would be done anyway without him. Noddy would play bass instead.

Noddy defends the recording as a great tight rock recording, which it is.
But as a *Slade* record?
Well, you decide.

20th
Don threw his copies of the Okey Cokey 45 straight in the bin.

30th
Jim's version of When The Lights Are Out was Paul Burnett's Record of the Week on BBC Radio 1.

Don went to Portland Studios. John Richards (drummer with The Rubettes) was 'mixing' some stuff there.

DECEMBER 1979

The Dummies – Jim Lea and his brother Frank – released a single: When The Lights Are Out / She's The Only Woman. It was said at the time (by Frank Lea) that they recorded the song as a joke, but soon became serious about it and so it was released.

The record picked up some radio plays and was a 1000 copy pressing. 300 were made available via the fan newsletter.

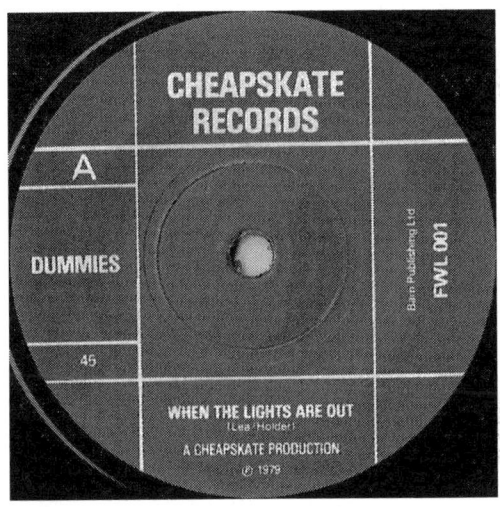

Monday 3rd - Slade rehearsal - John Henry's rehearsal studio, Holloway.

Friday 7th - St Bart's Hospital - London (private function)

The single Okey Cokey / My Baby's Got It was released on Barn 011. Some promo copies were pressed up by RSO, but the company didn't get as far as actually releasing the record officially. A proposed deal that had been discussed with management as far back as January of this year didn't ever get signed. Presumably, details couldn't be worked out.

Don Powell said that he threw his copies away. The barn records release got to number 83 on the charts.

SLADE'S NEW SINGLE IS A MUST FOR EVERY PARTY 'OKEY COKEY

BARN 011

SLADE: 'Okey Cokey' (Barn).
Yes, it's *that* one. Don't laugh; one day the Clash may be old men singing beer drinking songs on MFP. Let's hope not.

Saturday 8th - Goldsmiths College, London
Don Powell got his 'clean' driving licence back.

Tuesday 11th
Recording the 'backing track' for the 'Okey Cokey' 'Get It Together' TV show performance at Granada TV Manchester.

Tuesday 12th
Granada TV Manchester to record the 'Get It Together' TV show - miming to 'Okey Cokey' and 'My Baby's Got It.

Thursday 13th - Music Machine - Camden, London
Support: The Drill

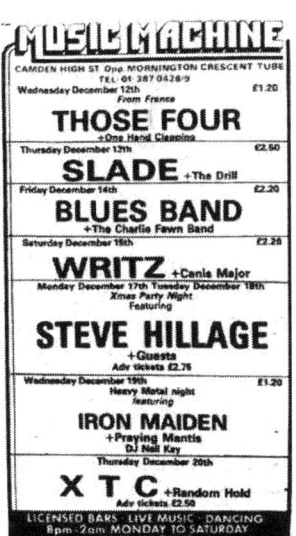

**SLADE
Music Machine, London**

OK YOU lot down there on the dance floor. Put your left foot in, take your left foot out, in out in out shake it all about, do the hokey cokey... Hey, this ain't rock 'n' roll, this is genocide! Folks are gonna get slayed!!

At any usual gig, perhaps, but this was different. After years in the wilderness, Slade are back. And you know something? They're as red hot 'n' lively as ever.

Sure, high-fringed Dave Hill has succumbed to the extra pound or seven, but is that gonna stop him leaping atop the PA to fire out glitter-best guitar licks? No sir, and at the other end Jim Lea is equally vicious, hammering out horrific violin licks as Don Powell crashes out torrents of mean rhythms.

But it's Noddy that the fans love and our own Mr Holder looks as young and fit as ever as he goads them on with his hooligan wide boy charm. Crashing out chords and orchestrating the headbanging, Slade give the impression that they were the prototype Quo. A hard-thumping dance band for those rockers freshly spilt from the football terraces.

A far cry from the contemporary tribalism of today's gigs. It read, a sociable we're-all-having-fun-together attitude, with the revellers united in the common cause of coming to feel the noise.

And noise was what we got, not to mention a great display of party hats, balloons and flashing lights. There were the old hits, 'Mama Weer Orl Crazee Now', 'Gudbuy T'-Jaine' (all mis-spellings approximate) 'Get Down And Get With It,' 'Everyday' and of course, a rousing, almost tear-jerking 'Merry Xmas Everybody'.

Will Slade be restored to their former glory or are they just half-forgotten heroes? It's anybody's guess but judging by this performance, a good chunk of their fans have already received one Christmas gift they won't forget in a hurry.

MIKE NICHOLLS

Don bought some new drum equipment before their show, which was attended by a number of luminaries from the rock world, including writer Chris Charlesworth.

Saturday 15th
The group drove to Birmingham Airport to fly to Guernsey. Swinn called to say the gig was off. The ferry couldn't leave with their equipment due to severe gales. Slade would have to go there the next week. Don Powell was now able to attend his Dad's birthday party.

Friday 21st
The group drove to Southampton to record the backing tracks for 'Okey Cokey' and 'Merry Christmas Everybody' which were to be used on the Saturday Banana TV show the following day at Southern TV.

Saturday 22nd
Beau Sejjour,
Guernsey.

Support:
The Brakes / Lurkers / Streetcar

Slade recorded their appearance on the 'Saturday Banana' TV show, then they flew to Guernsey.

Wednesday 26th
Slade's appearance on 'Get It Together' was broadcast.

LONDON

9.30 CARTOON TIME (rpt.).
9.35 UNTAMED FRONTIER : Winter.
10.0 SIMON IN THE LAND OF CHALK DRAWINGS (rpt.)
10.10 PIPKINS : Puppet programme.
10.25 GET IT TOGETHER : Pop show with Roy North, Linda Fletcher and guests Rosetta Stone, Lesley Duncan, The Original Mirrors, Slade and the ELO.
11.0 CARTOON TIME.

*Simon In The Land Of Chalk Paintings. Classic TV.
If you didn't get it outside London, you REALLY lost out.*

It's back to base for Noddy & Co.

IF any group has done enough this decade to ensure its place in rock 'n' roll history, Slade has.

Not that these Midland heavy rockers considered they are ready to be consigned to the history books yet.

It's true that since the heady days of 1973 when they registered no fewer than three number one hits - taking their total to six - their name has hardly been on everyone's lips. Nor have tht had a major hit single for two years.

Their self-imposed exile in America saw the end of 'a.lade as a British hit machine. But their contribution to rpck was greater than their famous boncy records with the misspelled titles.

They were one of the inspirations of the new wave that crashed over the industry two years ago.

Dave, Noddy, Don and Jimmy have all now returned tolive in their native Midlands, and to celebrate they have released a new album, Return To Base.

Guitarist Dave Hill was in a reflective mood when Icalled to discuss this latest attempt at a big-time come-back.

"A lot of the bands now making their names tell us we were theirfirst heroes swhen they were kids. And it seems a number of the new wavers first started playing instruments after listening to us."

The band still draws crowds and is hardly abort of work. Recently they went into cabaret style night clubs.

"We don't regard thaat as a graveyard for rock groups," says Dave. "Bands like Showaddywaddy are remarkably successful there. "it was a lot of fun and we didn't tone down our act. We were attracting all kinds of people, even businessmen."

Slade are shareholders in their record compan, Barn, and thoughcomfortably off, much of their money is invested in their music.

Dave is not worried by the current state of the music business.

"In our heyday youngsters were into the cult thing. They followed theur favourite group and stuck to them. Tastes are more catholic now.

For instance, I believe our last chart topper, Merry Christmas Everybody, was the last record to go straight into the charts at number one."

Return To Base may not have the impact a Slade album would have had a few years ago. But it shows that while the style remains distinctive, the group's expertise has grown.

Noddy Holder's unique, rasping vocals still power out a good rock song.

The playing is raucous and exciting. And it gets its mainmessage asross. Rock 'n' roll is nothing if it isn't fun.

JANUARY 1980

11th: The Dummies single was issued on the Pye label, but didn't chart.

THE DUMMIES

Paul Faulkner had played guitar on the B-side and would make it onto the picture sleeve of the reissue single, along with Frank and Jim.

PRESS INFORMATION

THE DUMMIES

The Dummies are a studio band and the brainchild of Frank Lea, brother of Slade's Jim Lea.

In 1975, Frank stood in for Don Powell (drummer in Slade) when Don was in hospital following his tragic car accident.

Afterwards Frank found himself with the urge to become a pro musician. He toured Europe, Scandinavia and the U.K. in various bands before deciding to give up live performances in favour of studio work. At the same time he formed his own company, Cheapskate Productions.

For "When The Lights Are Out", he called on his brother's talent and experience as a guide to his first solo project.

Jim Lea has been involved in 24 hit singles (7 No. 1's) as both songwriter and performer, also 8 hit albums (4 No. 1's). Apart from accolades too numerous to mention, he has also earned three Ivor Novello awards for services to the music industry.

"When The Lights Are Out" received immediate national airplay on release and was chosen by Paul Burnett as his record of the week.

Frank see's studio ideas in action as opposed to slogging on the road as the 80's way of approaching the music industry.

RELEASE DATE: 11TH JANUARY 1980

PYE POPULAR 7P 163   THE DUMMIES   "When The Lights Are Out"/She's The Only Woman

PYE RECORDS PRESS OFFICE
JANUARY 1980

SLADE

SLADE have set the following concerts as part of their comeback campaign: Watford Town Hall (February 28), London Music Machine (29, March 1), Cardiff University (4), Norwich Cromwells (6), Reading Charles Hall (7), St Austell Cornish Riviera (8), Stockton Fiesta (10), London Marquee (11) and Jersey Beham (14, 25).

ISSUE 6

Thursday 28th - Town Hall, Hempstead Road, Watford.
Support: The Drill

Friday 29th - Music Machine. High Street, Camden, London
Support: The Drill

Audio exists from this show.

Hear Me Calling / My Baby Left Me / When I'm Dancin' I Ain't Fightin' / Take Me Bak 'Ome / Wheels Ain't Coming Down / Lemme Love Into You / Everday / Somethin' Else / Pistol Packin' Mama / Night Starvation / Gudbuy T'Jane / Dizzy Mama / Get Down And Get With It / Mama Weer All Crazee Now / Cum On Feel The Noize / I'm A Rocker / Boney Maroney.

MARCH 1980
Saturday 1st - Music Machine. High Street, Camden, London
Support: The Drill
Audio exists from this show.

Hear Me Calling / My Baby Left Me / When I'm Dancin' I Ain't Fightin' / Take Me Bak 'Ome / Wheels Ain't Coming Down / Lemme Love Into You / Everday / Somethin' Else / Pistol Packin' Mama / Night Starvation / Gudbuy T'Jane / Dizzy Mama / Get Down And Get With It / Mama Weer All Crazee Now / Cum On Feel The Noize / I'm A Rocker / Born To Be Wild.

Tuesday 4th - University - Cardiff, Wales

Thursday 6th - Cromwell Club. Edward Street, Norwich

Friday 7th – St Charles Hall, Reading.

Saturday 8th - New Cornish Riviera Club. Carlyon Bay, St Austell.
Support: The Drill

Monday 10th - Fiesta Club, Norton Road, Stockton on Tees.

Tuesday 11th - Marquee Club, Wardour Street, London.
Support: The Drill

Friday 14th - Behan's Club, St Aubyns Rd, Jersey.

Saturday 15th - Behan's Club. St Aubyns Rd .Jersey.

Tuesday 25th - Behan's Club, St Aubyns Rd, Jersey.

Sunday 20th April – Zurich, Switzerland

MAY 1980

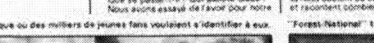

23rd: The Six Of The Best EP appeared on Chas Chandler's Six Of The Best label. SUPER45-3. Jim Lea was credited with the 'design' for the sleeve, which was basically a set of black lines across a white background.

Not all of the tracks on the EP were new. Three of them were from the Return To Base album from the previous year. But at a mere £1.49, the buyer could hardly grumble.

Night Starvation was a catchy, upbeat and memorable rocker, which made it to their stage show and stayed there for quite some time. Clever call and response vocals and cheeky innuendo in the lyrics. Naughty but nice.

When I'm Dancin' I ain't Fightin' was an excellent track too. Maybe a bit similar in structure and chord sequence to Let's Spend The Night Together by the Rolling Stones, but sped up and with an irresistible chorus and intro vocals. Another one that remained in their stage show.

I'm A Rocka was excised from Return To Base and it fits in well on the 'Rock Side' of this disc. Another one that graced their live shows.

The 'Back side' of the disc contained Don't Waste Your time (Back Seat Star) and Wheels Ain't Comin' Down. The song Nine To Five was a fast song that probably could have been a hit for another act – not that there is anything at all wrong with the Slade recording. Great lyrics, with a catchy and very commercial tune.

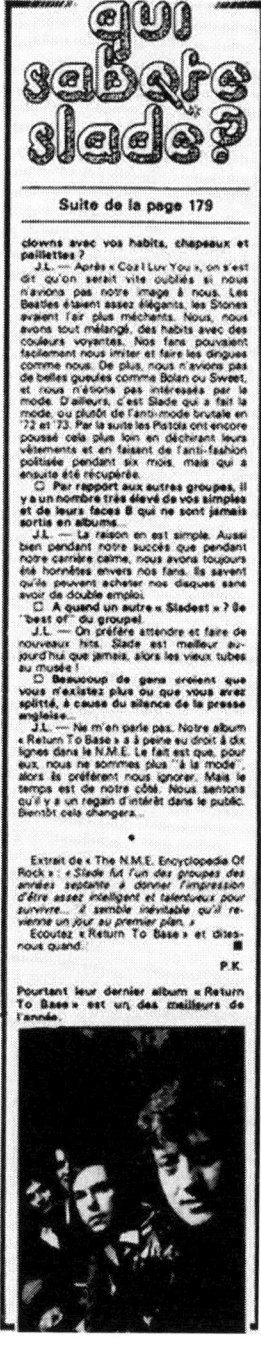

45 REVOLUTION

CHAS CHANDLER, a member of the original Animals and more recently the head of Barn Records, is hoping to revolutionise the albums and singles market ... with a new concept he believes could make both redundant!

His plan is to release a series of 12" 45 rpm records — each containing six tracks and known as "Super 45's." The series will be entitled 'Six Of The Best' and Chandler hopes to keep the price stable at £1.49.

"Both the album and the single are out of date in my opinion," he told RECORD MIRROR. "I've always thought the single was too restrictive, and the album has become too expensive.

"My idea is to give buyers six titles to choose from. It'll then be up to radio stations to choose *their* favourite track."

The first 'Super 45' will be out next month, featuring En Route, and one featuring Slade should follow shortly afterwards. 'Super 45's' should then follow at fortnightly intervals.

SLADE
Night Starvation Etc (Six of the Best Super 45 — 3, Pye). Rasping guitar, spot-on Holder vocals, earthy and commercial, catchy riff. Six cuts, no duffs. Slade are no has-beens.

Night Starvation and When I'm Dancin' I ain't Fightin' were the first plug tracks and were put out on a 7" promo single. Another, far scarcer, 7" plug disc featured Nine To Five / Don't Waste Your time (Back Seat Star).

A copy of the last disc featuring Don't Waste My time / I'm A Rocker has been seen, but I cannot swear to its authenticity..

Slade set to burst back into charts

POP by John Ogden

A CONFIDENT-SOUNDING Slade are all set for a big attempt to get back into the charts with the release of a special disc containing six songs for only £1.49.

Three of the songs are new, and the others are remixed versions of the pick of the band's Return To Base album. Even fans who bought the album will find the disc a bargain.

Featured track — the one that gets all the radio plugs — is a song called Night Starvation, which deals fairly graphically with one of the lead vocalist Noddy Holder's pre-occupations — sex.

It fairly stomps along, but I'm afraid that the too-basic lyrics count against it. There are no rude words, I hasten to add, it's just a bit too unsubtle in this day and age.

Image

However, it is the sort of song which has made Slade so popular in the past, and it carries on Nod's lascivious but humourous image well enough.

I'd have preferred to see another new song, 9 to 5, getting the plays. This is a song which chugs along nicely in an almost rockabilly rhythm, and is sung in a light-hearted manner which comes off well. Nowhere near as frantic as Night Starvation, it exudes a far better spirit.

The third new song, When I'm Dancin I Ain't Fightin, also makes a good listen. It's got a rowdy background of cheering to it, and thumps along in style. It also shows plenty of imagination in the arrangements.

The three other tracks, which have all benefitted from re-mixing, nevertheless show what a good album Return To Base was.

The excellent Don't Waste Your Time, with its Garth Hudson-type organ sound; the out-and-out rock and roll sound of an old Chuck Berry number I'm A Rocka, and the equally fine Wheels Ain't Comin Down, which proves such a show-stopper on live gigs, all demonstrate Slade at their best — entertaining, amusing, and full of energy.

The record cover was designed by bassist Jimmy Lea which, after his involvment with The Dummies, leaves little in the record business that he hasn't now tried.

JUNE 1980

Press ad placed by their promotions company, Rime Enterprises, who circulated the promo discs for Six of The Best..

ROCK SIDE
NIGHT STARVATION
WHEN I'M DANCIN I AIN'T FIGHTIN
I'M A ROCKA

BACK SIDE
DON'T WASTE YOUR TIME
THE WHEELS AIN'T COMING DOWN
9 TO 5

SLADE TOUR JUNE '80

- 12th CEDAR CLUB, BIRMINGHAM.
- 13th LEEDS UNIVERSITY.
- 14th UNIVERSITY COLLEGE, LONDON.
- 15th WEBBINGTON COUNTRY CLUB.
- 18th NORBRECK CASTLE HOTEL.
- 19th WINTER GARDENS, CLEETHORPES.
- 20th MUSIC MACHINE, LONDON.
- 21st MUSIC MACHINE, LONDON.
- 23rd MARQUEE CLUB, LONDON.
- 24th ROCK GARDEN, MIDDLESBROUGH.
- 26th MINERS WELFARE CLUB, HUCKNALL.
- 27th SWANSEA UNIVERSITY.
- 28th WEST RUNTON, PAVILLION.

Thursday 12th - Cedar Club. Constitution Hill, Birmingham.

THE CEDAR CLUB
Constitution Hill
Birmingham
Tonight, June 12th
SLADE
★★★★★★★★★★★★★★
Friday 13th
GINGER BAKERS ENERGI
★★★★★★★★★★★★★★
Thursday 19th
ECHO & THE BUNNYMEN
★★★★★★★★★★★★★★
Friday 20th
PSYCHEDELIC FURS
★★★★★★★★★★★★★★
8.30 till 2 am
No Dress Restrictions

Friday 13th - Leeds University.
Support: Confessor
The very same hall where The Who recorded their Live At Leeds album.

LUU BONANZA ROCK, JAZZ & BLUES FRI JUNE
13th 1980. 7.30pm

SPECIAL GUESTS

SLADE

BOOK NOW.

ALSO — City Limits, Confessor, The Switch, The Vye, Shake Appeal, Spyder Blues Band, Blues Express, Garry Boyle, Nervosa + Stompers DISCO.

TICKETS £2
On Door.

BOOK NOW. Bar Extension till 1·00 a.m.
Doors Open 7·30 pm. · HOT FOOD!
All Proceeds to Charity
FRIDAY, JUNE 13, 7·30pm.

From the photo archive of Ian Edmundson

Saturday 14th - University College, London.
Sunday 15th - Webbington Country Club. Barton Rd, Axbridge.

Wednesday 18th - Norbreck Castle. Queens Promenade, Blackpool

Thursday 19th - Winter Gardens, Kingsway, Cleethorpes.

SOLID Entertainments

Presents

- SLADE -

+

Support and Disco

AT: WINTER GARDENS, KINGSWAY CLEETHORPES
THURSDAY 19th JUNE 1980, 8 p.m.- MIDNIGHT.

ADVANCE TICKET (Inc. V.A.T.) £2.50
ON THE DAY (Inc. V.A.T.) £3.00

Nº 0805　　　　　Nº 0805

Friday 20th - Music Machine, High St, Camden, London.
Support: Broken Home

Broken Home contained members of the group Mr Big who had a hit single with 'Romeo'.

Saturday 21st - Music Machine, High St, Camden, London.
Support: Broken Home

MUSIC MACHINE

CAMDEN HIGH ST Opp MORNINGTON CRESCENT TUBE
TEL 01 387 0428/9

Wednesday 11th June — £1.20
SPLODGENESSABOUNDS
+ Twits + Car Park

Thursday 12th June — £1.20
PROTEX & RENT BOYS

Friday 13th June — £2.20
BOYS
+ The Spicers

Saturday 14th June — £2.20
NEW MUZIK
+ Never Never Band

Monday 16th June — £1.20
NIK TURNERS INNER CITY UNIT
+ The Pack

Tuesday 17th June — £1.20
LONESOME NO MORE
+ Life Style
+ The Andy Blade Band

Wednesday 18th June — £1.20
WITCHFYNDE
+ More & Gaskin

Friday 20th June
SLADE
+ Broken Heart
Pay At Door £2.50

Saturday 21st June
SLADE
+ Broken Heart
Pay At Door £2.50

Saturday 28th June
PSYCHEDELIC FURS
+ SOFT BOYS
Pay At Door £2.50

LICENSED BARS · LIVE MUSIC · DANCING
8pm - 2am MONDAY TO SATURDAY
OVER 18s ONLY

Monday 23rd – Marquee, Wardour Street, London.
Support: Broken Home

⭐ Sun 22nd June (Adm £1.50)
MERTON PARKAS
Plus friends & Mandy H

Mon 23rd June (Adm £2)

S L A D E

Plus friend & Jerry Floyd

⭐ Tues 24th June (Adm £2)
THE LAMBRETTAS
Plus guests & Jerry Floyd

⭐ Wed 25th June (Adm £1.50)
THE Q TIPS
Plus support & Jerry Floyd

⭐ Thurs 26th June (Adm £1.50)
NEIL INNES
Plus friends & Jerry Floyd

Fri 27th & Sat 28th June (Adm £1.50)
R & B Special
9 BELOW ZERO
Plus support & D.J. Ian Fleming

⭐ Sun 29th June (Adm £1.50)
MERTON PARKAS
Plus friends & Mandy H

⭐ Mon 30th June (Adm £1.50)
GIRLSCHOOL
Plus support & Jerry Floyd

Don't Miss Our
Summer Residencies with
⭐ Weds: THE Q TIPS

Wednesday 25th - Pavilion. North Parade Road, Bath.

Thursday 26th – Hucknall & Linby Miners Welfare Club – Hucknall.
Radio Trent hosted the concert and recorded the event for broadcast.

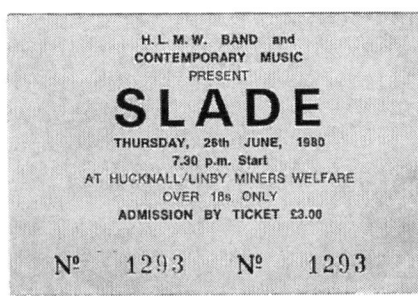 

From the book
SIX YEARS ON THE ROAD

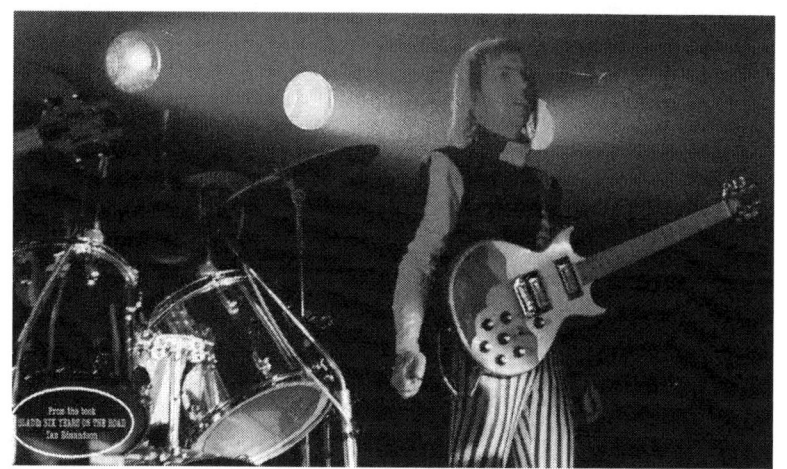

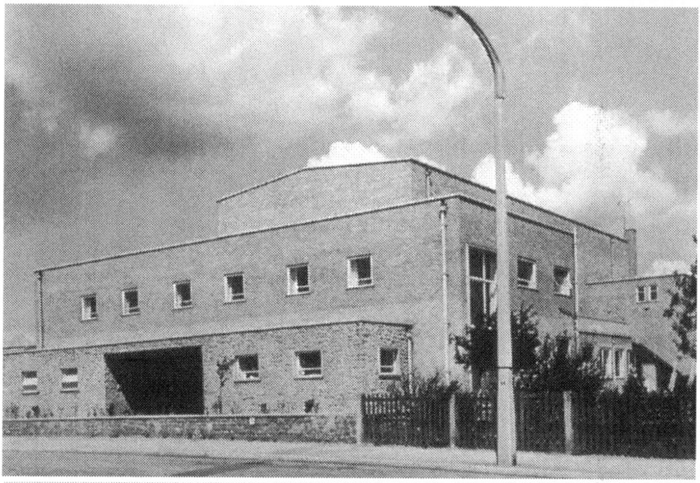

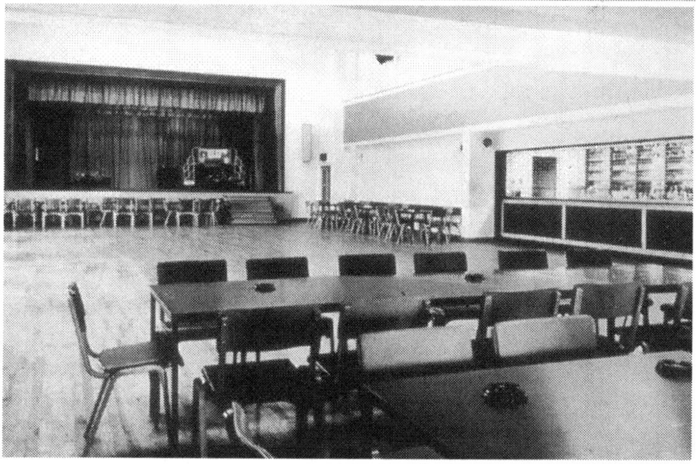

Saturday 28th June 1980 - Pavilion West Runton

Thursday 19th June	Great Hitmakers — **STEVE HARLEY AND COCKNEY REBEL**	Adv. Tickets £2·00
Saturday 21st June	As evy as they come — **BUDGIE**	Adv. Tickets £2·00
Saturday 28th June	The spirit of entertainment **SLADE**	Adm. £2·00 Members £1·80
Friday 11th July	**HAWKWIND**	Adv. Tickets £2·00
Saturday 12th July	EVYER THAN EVAR **SAMPSON + SLEDGEHAMMER**	£1·50 (members 50p off)
Thursday 17th July	Wayne Kennedy's **FLASH CATS** Great Rock + Roll night	

The group took some time off after this. No plans were made to regroup. It later came out in interviews that Dave Hill was apparently so utterly dejected by the state of Slade's fortunes that he had actually left the group. They didn't tell anyone.

AUGUST 1980
Musicians Only carried an interview with Noddy Holder.

SLADE

Whatever happened to them?
Tony Horkins finds out

TAKE THE average 'established' musician aside and he'll tell you he was weaned on the likes of Beck, Clapton, and Hendrix. On the other hand the younger bands only think of Cream as the stuff they pour over their strawberries. There are those of us that spent a great proportion of our childhood chanting such profound statements as 'Come On, Come On', 'We want Sweet', or, more to the point, 'Mama Weer All Crazee Now'. Whatever did happen to Slade?

Slade's phenomenal success came in 1971 with the release of 'Cos I Luv You' and lasted a full five years. Nowadays if you want to catch the band you just pop down to the local poly, but then it was Earls Court. Unless you happen to be an English teacher, you probably liked either 'Take Me Bak 'Ome', 'Cum On Feel The Noize' or maybe 'Gudbuy T'Jane'? In the offices of Keith Altham Publicity I ask Noddy Holder in 1980 'What have Slade been doing during the last five years?'

'We've been working just as hard... TOURING!'

But what happens to a band that reaches such a high target as Slade did and then just disappears?

'Well, we'd had six years of huge success, 18 hit singles and about seven hit albums, made the movie and we felt, as a band, we were getting stale.

'We'd bring a new single out, it would go in the charts, we'd do the same touring over Europe and Australia, and we felt that if we didn't make a break... we've always been a good live band and we just weren't enjoying it anymore. So, we decided to go to America.'

So in the middle of '75 they made their way over to the land of fortune to break new ground. For two years they tried to crack it but didn't really have any luck.

'We couldn't get any AM radio play, which is the singles market, because they thought we were too rowdy. We got much more FM play and sold more albums which helped the live thing.'

By the time they'd come back refreshed in '77 things had changed within the music business and bands were gigging regularly again. 'It really gave us the urge to get out on the road and slog at it again.'

Then they released the album 'Whatever Happened To Slade?', followed by 'Slade Live Volume 2' and started hauling themselves over Europe again. But don't start queueing outside Earls Court again just yet, try the Marquee. 'I'm sure a lot of people are under the impression that once you've made a hit single that's it — a house in the country, a dog by your side and Britt Ekland curled up on the rug.

'A lot of the new young bands come and see us in the dressing room after a gig for a chat. They're groups that have had one or two records in the charts and they're already talking as if they're set up for life financially. It just don't work like that, but you can't tell them. You can't just say to them "You're not going to make a fortune out of two hit singles". Especially if they've had advances and have already spent the money on touring and buying equipment. That all comes out of the royalties.'

So how much success do you need before you start pulling in the readies?

'It varies. If you have a hit single that's a top twenty hit in Britain alone it's not enough. You're going to need a few of them, especially if you're touring expensively. Touring has got to be financed from somewhere.

'To start making money you've got to talk about three or four decent hit records. You make more money if you write the numbers yourself but to start seeing any great rewards you've got to have world-wide hits.'

One way of trying to get those records in the charts is to sell your art. Nowadays the special limited edition album for £3.99 is a pretty common sight, the EP is back and, in Slade's case, a six-track, twelve-inch single for £1.49 is the bait. Call one of the numbers the 'featured track' and you're in business. The package is on manager Chas Chandler's label, appropriately called 'Six Of The Best Records'.

'You're never going to get the case where the record company has cut back on the price and cut their profits, it's really got to be down to the artist. We haven't released one good track and five rubbish ones but six strong tracks. It's a new idea, an experiment, and we haven't seen the rewards of it yet.

'We were able to record it cheaply as we used Chas's studio which helps to cut the cost which is one of the reasons why we can sell it cheaper. If the idea works it's giving the public real good value for money. You're getting half an album for £1.49.'

So why can't a whole album be made for under £3? 'Don't ask me. The groups have got to take a lesser cut for a start, and the group can't do that unless the record company do it as well. We're lucky that ours will. You're cutting your profit margin quite considerably but it's got to be a mutual thing with your record company.'

To cut your record profits in Slade's early days would have been easier, as it didn't cost quite so much to get out on the road.

'In those days we went out on the road with very little equipment. I had a Vox AC30, Dave the guitarist had a Vox AC30, Jim the bass player had an 18in Selmer bass cabinet with a 50 Watt top, Don had just a small drum kit and we had our own PA. That had four 12in speakers in cabinets each side with the amp all in one that worked from the stage. You didn't have a sound guy out front. And we all used to travel in an old J2 van with all the equipment and we had one roadie at that time. He didn't get paid but he'd do it for the fun of it. He's our personal tour manager now.

'With that size of equipment you could play theatres quite easily in those days. The same backline but with a PA column each side and you'd be playing Hammersmith Odeon. But that was loud then. It's only over the years that groups started to build bigger and bigger gear and now unless you go into a place that's got huge stacks of gear you're disappointed. It's what you're used to.'

Do you think that sort of equipment line-up will do these days? 'Not in a theatre, but in the clubs, yes. Bands that start out hiring big PAs and lights and things are throwing money down the drain really. You can have a small backline and PA and if the band's "got it" they don't need a big light system. We've got a very small lighting rig, but we use what we've got to great effect.'

Are you still using Vox AC30s?

'Oh no, we use Hi-Watts now, but we only use a stack each, though we do have spares on the stage of everything. Me and Dave use a Hi-Watt 200 stack each, but Jim uses a very huge system of bins for the bass and Hi-Watts for his top sound. He's got much more powerful gear than we have.'

Why's that?

'Because he likes to get a cross-section of sound. He likes the bottom really coming out of the bins but his style of playing also calls for a lot of top. He does sort of lead playing on the bass as well, so he has to have a very toppy sound mixed in.'

As for guitars, Dave and Jim use John Birch and JD guitars (JD used to work with John Birch) with their on pickups on, and Noddy uses Gibson Juniors with JD and John Birch pickups on them.

Slade's five year jaunt at the top seemed long in comparison to today's bands. Nowadays a band comes and goes about two months. Why does Noddy think that is?

'I think the musical climate is different. There's a huge turnover of bands — there's loads and loads of them. There's always been a lot of bands but in the time that we were making it you had to be very strong live to survive. At the time there were very few bands touring consistently. Nowadays there's loads of bands touring and there's a saturation which creates this huge turnover.'

Which, as Noddy so rightly points out, is not such a bad thing. Those who have their heart in being in a band will stick it out, and the people that do it to make a quick buck won't.

'Hopefully you'll be left at the end of the day with the genuine rock and rollers,' ends Noddy wistfully.

8th: A second outing for The Dummies Didn't You Used To Used To Be You / Miles Out To Sea is released as a single on the independent Cheapskate label. CHEAP3.

Pick of the week

THE DUMMIES: "Didn't You Use To Be Use To Be You?" (Cheapskate). Whatever happened to Slade? Well, half of them wrote this, and it's terrific. A moral tale of the fleeting fame of one Harry Higgins, a one-hit wonder who looks much taller on TV! Shifting rhythms, witty lyrics and a storming chorus. Deserves all it gets.

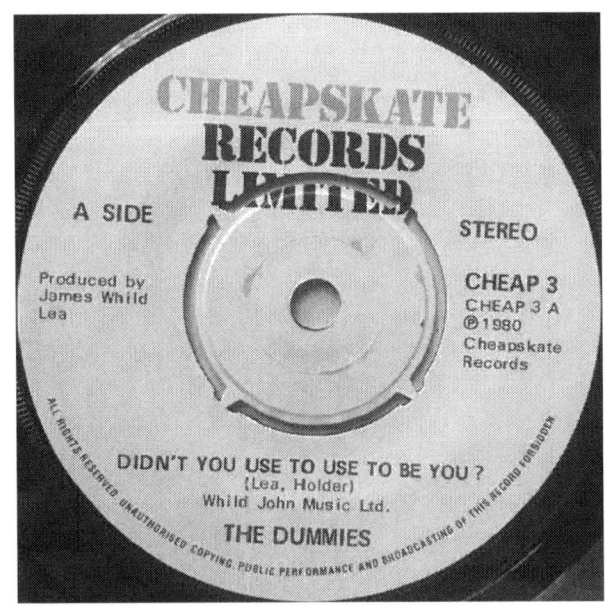

This was a burst of pure energy, compared to some of the recent Slade releases and it is just astonishing that they didn't use this Holder / Lea song themselves. However, Slade were effectively dormant when this single was recorded and released, so perhaps there was actually not a Slade left to record it. It was a small radio hit and Jim Frank and Louise appeared on TV to promote it. It was originally titled 'One Hit Wonder' and I have an acetate disc from Portland Studio which uses that title.

The B-side was an interesting re-make of the Slade song from Old New Borrowed And Blue.

HOT TOP 20

Il y a deux semaines	PLACES	TITRES	INTERPRETES	Points	Semaines
2	1	LP « RETURN TO BASE »	Slade	461	12
1	2	LP « PETER GABRIEL »	Peter Gabriel	450	10
19	3	EP « SIX OF THE BEST »	Slade	315	4
6	4	« LOVE WILL TEAR US APART »	Joy Division	305	4
—	5	LP « CLOSER »	Joy Division	290	2
5	6	LP « FROM A TO B »	New Muzik	289	10
7	7	« OVER YOU »	Roxy Music	282	8
15	8	LP « EMPTY GLASS »	Pete Townshend	279	10
3	9	LP « FLESH + BLOOD »	Roxy Music	279	10
14	10	LP « DIANA »	Diana Ross	277	4
4	11	LP « TRAVELOGUE »	The Human League	271	10
11	12	« VISCO VIDEO »	The Bowling Balls	252	16
—	13	DLP « ONE OF THE ROAD »	Kinks	239	4
18	14	« CHRISTINE »	Siouxsie + The Banshees	235	4
12	15	LP « EMOTIONAL RESCUE »	Rolling Stones	226	6
20	16	LP « REAL PEOPLE »	Chic	208	4
17	17	LP « XANADU »	Original Soundtrack	208	4
16	18	LP « NEUROVISION »	Telex	186	16
—	19	LP « CULTORUS ERECTUS »	Blue Oyster Cult	185	2
10	20	LP « THE GAME »	Queen	184	10

● ceux qui montent.

That August, Slade were quite happily perched at number one and number three on the Belgian Telemustique charts.
Sunday 31st

Reading Festival
Also on the bill: Whitesnake, Def Leppard, Gary Moore, Magnum, Budgie, Girl, etc.

As is now well-known, Ozzy Osbourne's band Blizzard Of Ozz withdrew from the bill of the Reading Festival, as Ozzy had reportedly said they weren't really ready for it. Other Ozzy dates were cancelled.

The Marquee Club organised the annual event and approached Chas Chandler regarding Slade filling the vacant slot on the last night of the festival. He called the band, who discussed it amongst themselves, and all but Dave Hill readily agreed to do it. He was still totally disillusioned with Slade and wanted no part of any more shows.

Chas Chandler turned up at his doorstep, towered over him *(but everyone towers over Dave Hill)* and persuaded him to at least let the band go to Reading and for him to finish with the band on a high note, instead of their last gig having been held at West Runton Pavilion.

The Slade slot was announced on the 23rd of August.

The band drove down to Reading in one car, parked on the public car park, as they had no passes or permits and walked with their guitars, through the milling crowds to get to the stage entrance. Their names, of course were not on the list, but they were finally admitted and found their dressing area backstage. Various people came to visit them and wish them well and reassured them that they would 'smash it' on the day.

Def Leppard, who had recently supported them, insisted on going higher up the bill from Slade, as they were a band on the way up and didn't want to go beneath 'a bunch of has-beens'. Slade didn't argue the toss.

They just went out and they did their business, as usual.

G-FORCE OUT

THE FINAL CHANGES have been announced for this year's Reading Festival
  IN come Slade (!), White Spirit and Angelwitch and OUT go Angel City, G-Force and Blizzard of Ozz Don't forget the wellies and the plastic bags.

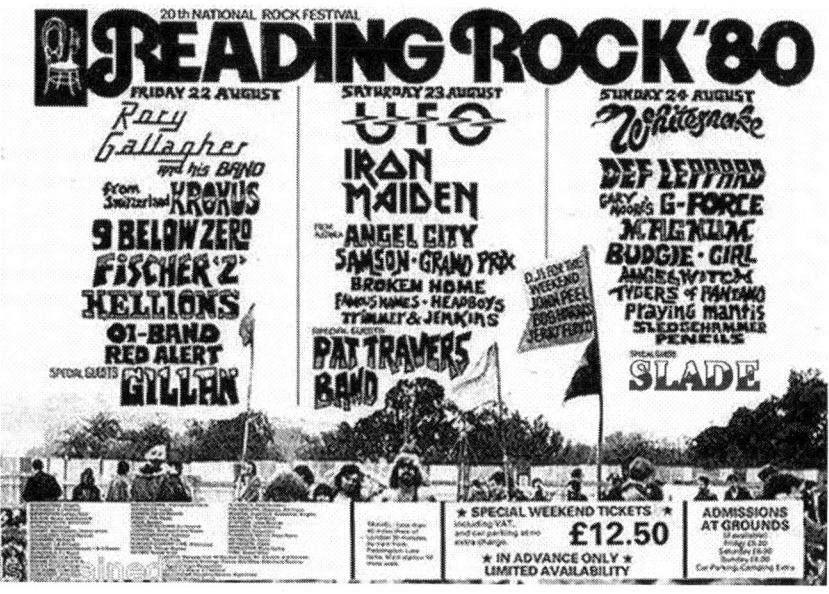

Dizzy Mama; My Baby Left Me; Take Me Bak 'Ome; When I'm Dancin' I Ain't Fightin'; Wheels Ain't Coming Down; Everyday; Somethin' Else / Pistol Packin' Mama / Keep a Rollin'; You'll Never Walk Alone (crowd singalong); Mama Weer All Crazee Now; Get Down And Get With It Merry Xmas Everybody (crowd singalong): Cum on Feel the Noize; Born to Be Wild.

An abbreviated 'highlights' disc from this show would be released in the All The World Is A Stage live box set in 2022. It is impossible to work out why BMG did not release the whole show.

When SLADE came on the crowd went wild. And rightly so. The band were marvellous, undoubtedly the success story of the festival. Take Me Back Home and Mama, We're All Crazy Now might be old favourites, but they were performed with such polish and professionalism, they seemed crisp and new. Bob Harris commented afterwards: "There's no substitute for experience and good songs." How right he was.
It was hard for the youngsters in DEF LEPPARD to follow that but they worked hard, providing a finer HM band than Iron Maiden the previous night and, despite a weak album, suggesting they'll go far.

Noddy Holder: "*We didn't know we were doing this fucking gig til' about three days ago.*"

Dave Hill: "*One heck of an experience, 'cos I wasn't going to do that gig. Slade manager Chas Chandler talked me into it...the confidence came when there was a reaction, as it built and built, sort of got bigger and bigger. I mean getting that lot to sing "Merry Xmas Everybody" was amazing. I could see Chas at the side grinning.*"

They went on as rank outsiders and at the end of the day, they were a band practically reborn. Def Leppard went on to face an exhausted crowd and, while they may not have exactly died a complete death, they came away realising their mistake in following Slade. The people who weren't tired out threw beer cans at them.

The newspaper reviews that followed were pleasing. The normally hostile press had no option but to say what the crowd reaction had been.

Thirteen years on and Budgie are still bashing away. Steve Williams laid down a beat that felt like a gin hangover while John Thomas and Burke Shelley added suitable embellishments — i.e., they pulverised the audience into a happy submission. If the early half of the afternoon represented the HM new wave with Sledgehammer, Praying Mantis, Angelwitch and the Tygers Of Pan Tang, the evening gave way to the old guard.

Whether Slade fall into the last category is open to dispute, old they are. They still have the same taste in circus clothing, Noddy Holder still does his bad impression of Lennon with tonsilitis, and Dave Hill totters around on fopish shoes while leaping on a big box. "Cum On Feel The Noise", "Merry Christmas" plus assorted hitlets were duly wheeled out and by the time they reached the appropriately titled "Mama We're All Crazy Now" they were received like Liverpool beating Everton at home. The lads even dared to throw toilet rolls at the masses — yes Slade drew the best response outside of headliners Whitesnake.

Def Leppard failed to hold the rabble's attention, so once again many returned to chucking cans, pausing only to flash peace signs during the endless guitar solos.

"I don't think there's anything wrong in throwing cans," remarked one of the festival's many young stewards, "just as long as they're not full or Party Sevens — my mate caught one of those in the head and needed 14 stitches."

Slade's Noddy Holder — re-emerging with style.

UNCLE NODDY Holder in feeble Bad Manners impersonation

BY SIX o'clock, the old age pensioners were becoming excited. **Budgie** were due on soon. Surprise, surprise, the old boys carried themselves off quite adequately which is to be expected since they were doing exactly the same when most of the NWOBHM invaders were merely learning how to play with their cardboard rattles. Even Budgie, though, were no competition for the other 'old men' of the evening, **Slade**, who carried a trophy of trashy magnificence too powerful for many to reject.

"What did you think of Slade?" came the questions, hither and thither, from festival people who hoped that they'd surely found something, *anything*, that might appeal to a journalist's pernickety palate. Well, yes chaps, I liked them. Slade were certainly far better than almost all of the HM garbage that'd been thrown at us for most of the weekend. Even Barton thought he'd found his paradise.

One show had changed everything for Slade. Behind the scenes, what was in truth a totally abandoned and empty work calendar was suddenly and hastily populated with lots of show dates.

Slade announced a string of dates with ex-Runaways guitarist Joan Jett as support. These gigs were highly anticipated, but Joan Jett found herself suddenly promoting a massive hit in America with her cover of *I Love Rock'N'Roll* and she was obliged to pull out of the Slade dates.

The replacement support on the tour was Straight Eight, former proteges of The Who's guitarist and principal songwriter, Pete Townshend.

Smart work by Noddy . . .

Rock star Noddy Holder — wearing unaccustomed suit and tie — steals a kiss from the bride at a Warley wedding.

The lead singer of the Wolverhampton-based group Slade was acting as best man at the marriage of the group's sound engineer Ian Newnham.

The group's other members, Dave Hill,

Jimmy Lea and drummer Don Powell were also guests at the wedding of Ian, of Brookside Close, Wombourne, and Miss Eileen Delahay, of Pitfields Road, Warley.

The couple were married at St Hubert's Roman Catholic Church on the Wolverhampton New Road, and left in style in a Model T Ford vintage car.

The ceremony was followed by a reception for 250 guests at Regis Hall, Reddal Hill Road, Old Hill.

SEPTEMBER 1980

Saturday 6th - St Gerard Rock Festival - Belgium

Photo: Luc Rossini.

20th: Sounds.
The lesson of this next image is ALWAYS be careful who you agree to share a stage with...

Due to the late discovery of the horrible antics of the disgraced BBC DJ – the beastly Jimmy Savile - a huge number of Top Of The Pops appearances will never ever be shown on television ever again, as he introduced a number of the groups and he's not exactly welcome on television anymore.

This probably affects the prospect of a commercial release of any of this Slade footage too.

Jim (and Jim and Jim) will fix it

WE THREE wish to impart to you our spiritually enlightening experience at the recent Reading Festival. Our trio arrived in eager anticipation of exhilarating live music — only to experience five days (FIVE days? — What were you on man? — Drugs Ed.) of dull, boring, heavy metal.

By Saturday night we were thoroughly disheartened with the whole idiom of Kerrang and on Sunday, awoken by the sun's penetrating the tent, we spent the morning close to the edge, down by the river (eh! eh!) thankful that we were not being subjected to the despicable tortures being administered to those poor deprived wretches in the area. Back in the arena for the late night "entertainment", we snored to the sound of the bands White Spirit, Magnum (urghhh, excuse me) praying for better things to come. We were not disappointed!!!

"Just as the sun creates external constancy, so the Slade represents the unchanging elements in the changing mind of man." — Xenopus Toad, Wolverhampton. Slade had arrived... From the back of the arena, three disenchanted humanoids accelerated from 0 to 60, beercan-arms aloft. We had seen the light. Slade were here. Is this the second coming? we shouted as 30,000 lost souls joined our rejoicing.

Presently Noddy spake unto us: "Reading, are you ready to RRRock?" and as the euphoric reception died down we were whisked away, we witnessed surely the greatest happening since the birth of Jimmy Page.

"The Slade is a window which we can neither look at or through, thus creating a total illusory image floating in a material world. Its implacable depths are the fast flowing rivers of the tunnel at the end of which the searcher's souls will be joined as one." — The Pozing Bozo, Ronald Reegan, Alberto Frog, Nortonwood, Stroud, Glos.

'DEAR JIM, please can you fix it for me to win the next General Election? Signed, Jim Callaghen'. Pictured above, the two man test Labour's new secret weapon, the Slade Revival, as personified by guitarist Jim Lea

Thursday 25th - New Webbington Country Club, Weston Super Mare
Friday 26th - Central London Poly. 115 New Cavendish St, London W1

P.C.L.S.U. PRESENTS

SLADE

Plus **SPECIAL GUESTS**

FRIDAY, 26th Sept. 8 till late. Bar

Poly of Central London
115 New Cavendish St., London W1
(Oxford Circus / Grt. Portland St. tube)

£1.50 Students. £2.50 others

On: 01-636 6271

27th: Wolverhampton Express & Star.

Encore for the forgotten men

Midlands rock band Slade are making a new start, as JOHN OGDEN reports

EVEN in the transitory world of rock and roll, history can repeat itself. Just ask Slade.

Dateline 1972: At the Lincoln rock festival a hard-working but little thought of band gets a grudging chance to play one of the support spots. Their energy, enthusiasm and cheery aggression earn them a standing ovation and make them the surprise hit of the festival.

They follow up with a hit record, and for the next two years are rarely out of the charts. Slade have arrived.

Dateline 1980: At the Reading rock festival one of the acts, The Blizzard of Oz, drops out. To replace them a hard-working but little thought of band gets a grudging chance to play the spot. Their energy, enthusiasm and cheery aggression earn them a standing ovation and make their act the highlight of the festival.

Slade, it seems, have arrived again! After six years "in the wilderness" one crowded hour upon the stage has once again made the Wolverhampton foursome into one of rock's hottest properties.

That brilliant show at Reading, where they faced an apathetic heavy rock audience and transformed it into a cheering, singing, clapping, joyful throng, has once again sent the concert promoters hunting them in droves, and the radio playing their songs again.

The music business has rediscovered what some of us have never forgotten: Few bands can put on a more enjoyable, hard-rocking good time concert than Slade.

Encores

The proof of the pudding is in the charts right now at No 44 and rising fast — an EP on the Cheapskate Label, recorded live at the concert by the BBC of Slade in full show-stopping flow. If anyone still doubts that they're back just listen to the roar of that audience!

The past few years haven't been all that bad for the band even so. They didn't have to change their act or go into cabaret to make a living as so many other declining groups have done.

They never went short of bookings — or encores at the end of the night — although the halls they played in were sometimes smaller and more out of the way, and the publicity was no longer there.

All it meant was that they couldn't get their songs played on the radio — but to many groups that's the kiss of death.

The difference with Slade was that even before Lincoln they had gathered a committed hard core of fans who knew they'd always get a good show when they went to see the band.

They stayed loyal during the good years and the lean ones that followed, and, combined with new ones who were curious about the group because of their past reputation, formed the basis for a steady living for Slade in the hitless yeas.

Even so it was highly frustrating for the group. Says bassist Jimmy Lea: "It was as though we were trapped in a vacuum bubble of our own success, in our music there are connections with punk, pop, and rock, but because we were really a bit of eveything we always seemed to be unfashionable."

109

So it was back on the road again, no longer guaranteed a seething full house, no longer imprisoned in besieged hotel rooms, no longer the automatic recipients of mass adulation.

It suited Jimmy down to the ground. "I like having to fight to make our audience accept us", he told me. "Our true fans were always there to make things go well, but it was the people standing at the back of the hall who we had to capture as well. That's the fight I enjoy.

"The others don't agree with me on this, but I think one of the worst times for us as a band was when we were No 1 all the time. I used to think, before all the fame, that the sign of success was when the audience went wild even before you went on stage, but when we did get that I didn't like it".

Better

But it was galling to see their records go into the top hundred regularly, then fail to get any higher because of lack of radio plays. As far as the broadcasters were concerned they were forgotten men.

Reading changed all that.

In a festival consisting almost entirely of declamatory, doom-laden heavy metal self-indulgence, Slade were a blast of fresh air.

They proved it's possible to have fun and still be able to slam out a thunderous piece of music; and, most of all, that "pop group" Slade could play tighter, heavier, and better than most of the other acts on the bill.

How did they feel, considering that the organisers were extremely reluctant to put them on the show at all?

Said Jimmy: "We never 'die' anywhere, so it was just a question of how successful we would be. The only worry was that some of the groups had been canned off (pelted with beer cans until they left the stage). We knew that the crucial moment would come as soon as we walked on stage. If the cans were going to come that's when it would be. But as soon as we went out there we received an enormous cheer and not one can came on, so it was in the bag really, and we felt really confident."

Media

Since the concert the reaction has been equally spectacular. Every show they have done since then has been a sell-out, and another concert tour for November has been quickly arranged. Polydor records plan to bring out a "Slade's Greatest Hits" album for Christmas, with heavy television advertising, and there will doubtless be a new single on the way before that.

Monday 29th - Rotters Club, St Johns Precinct, Liverpool.
Support: Straight 8

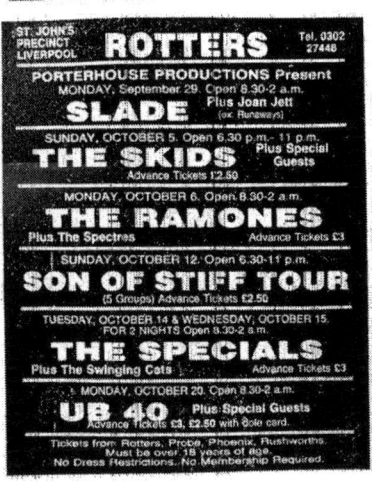

Nº 007

ST. JOHNS PRECINCT
LIVERPOOL Tel. 051-709-0771

Monday, 29th September   Open 8.30 p.m.
                          To 2.00 a.m.

Porterhouse Promotions Present

SLADE

PLUS JOAN JETT

Tickets £2.50 in advance
Must be over 18 years of age
THE MANAGEMENT RESERVE THE RIGHT TO REFUSE ADMISSION

Tuesday 30th - Rotters Club. Silver Street, Doncaster
Support: Straight 8

N⁰ 138

(SILVER STREET, DONCASTER)
Tel. 0302 27448

Tuesday, 30th September   Open 8.30p.m. To 2.00a.m.

Porterhouse Promotions Present

SLADE

PLUS JOAN JETT

Tickets £2.50 in advance

Must be over 18 years of age
THE MANAGEMENT RESERVE THE RIGHT TO REFUSE ADMISSION

Possibly the best string of gigs at any venue that I have ever seen.

STAR CHOICE

NODDY HOLDER — SLADE

1. WOMAN TO WOMAN Joe Cocker
2. WAITING FOR THE BUS ZZ Top
3. GET OUT OF DENVER Bob Seger
4. REASONS TO BE CHEERFUL
   Ian Dury and the Blockheads
5. SPEED KING Deep Purple
6. NEW YORK CITY John Lennon
7. ROXANNE Police
8. MERCEDES BENZ Janis Joplin
9. AIN'T NO LOVE IN THE HEART OF THE CITY Bobby Bland
10. NUAGES Django Reinhardt

OCTOBER 1980

Thursday 2nd - Fusion Club, Bridge Place, Aberdeen

Friday 3rd - Polytechnic, 2 Sandyford Road, Newcastle Upon Tyne

The Slade Alive At Reading EP was released on the independent Cheapskate Records label. CHEAP5.

After the press had had to admit to Slade's show-stealing performance, this EP, culled from a BBC broadcast of highlights of the show, could hardly fail to make some impression. Number 44 was not what they wanted, but it was a chart return and the EP got lots of radio plays. Slade were back.

SLADE: Alive at Reading '80 (Cheapskate)
Arguably the Reading success, it just goes to prove that Noddy and the lads are still a force in the world. The energy, precision — not to mention one of the great British rock voices at work — all go to make this live performance an object lesson to those new boys who would scorn hitmakers of earlier years. Buy now.

SLADE: "Alive At Reading '80" (Cheapskate). Aaah... *now* you're talking. Slade were the best out and out pop band of them all, bar *none*. They show they can still get a few asses wiggling with these four cuts from Reading, where they wiped the floor with Whitesnake, UFO et al by all accounts.

Noddy's throat could still saw through an oak tree and while their version of "Born To Be Wild" is pointless and the recording quality is a shade iffy, "When I'm Dancin' I Ain't Fightin' " is almost in the "Mama Weer All Crazee Now" class.

SURPRISE OF THE WEEK
SLADE: 'Alive At Reading' (EP) (Cheapskate) Ah, how soon we forgot. Recorded at this year's Reading mega-bore and rollicking fun in a kind of casualty ward way. Used to love 'Slayed Alive' I did and ...ah... the memories... Remember how wee used to spel awl owr wurds just lik the boize? Remember too how Britain's educationalists tore out their locks in fury and frustration as Slade maynee-a scoured the land. Noddy and the boys were, at one time, the greatest threat to the future of this country since the doodlebug. Shame that the plug track 'When I'm Dancin' I Ain't Fightin' ' although being Slade's manifesto for life, is also a shameless GBH job on 'Let's Spend The Night Together'. Also here you get a medly and 'Born To Be Wild' on which the Slades make not only Steppenwolf but all your macho strutting hipster metallic salesmen sound like... ohh... The Eagles with double medications in their tea and their surgical supports on the poolside table. Ineffably fab, and excuse me while I air and iron my old silk scarf.

SLADE MAKE HAY

SLADE, unexpectedly one of the hits of the recent Reading Festival, are releasing an EP of three tracks recorded live at that event. Titled 'Slade Alive At Reading 80', it's on Cheapskate Records and it comprises 'Something Else', 'Born To Be Wild' and 'When I'm Dancin' I Ain't Fightin'. The band also set out on the road next week for a 17-date tour, taking in:

Weston-super-Mare Webbington Club (September 25), London Central Polytechnic (26), Doncaster Rotters (29), Liverpool Rotters (30), Aberdeen Fusion (October 2), Newcastle Poly (3), Glasgow Queen Margaret Union (4), Cardiff University (6), Manchester University (8), Blackpool Norbreck Castle (9), Withernsea Grand Pavilion (10), Bradford University (11), Hardstoft Shoulder Of Mutton (13), Reading University (15), Nottingham Palais (16), Cromer West Runton Pavilion (17) and London Woolwich Thames Poly (18).

Saturday 4th - Queen Margaret Union. University Gardens, Glasgow

Monday 6th - University. Park Place, Cardiff, Wales

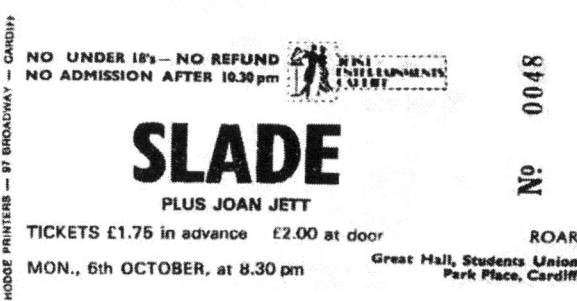

Wednesday 8th - University - Manchester
Support: Straight 8

Thursday 9th - Norbreck Castle Nitespot. Queens Parade, Blackpool
Support: Straight 8

The Norbreck Castle Nitespot show was again notable for Noddy Holder asking the bouncers to be a lot less heavy-handed with the audience. The result was almost the same as at their Porthcawl show some time before. Noddy Holder was on the receiving end of a punch from a bouncer after the show. Fortunately, he was not badly hurt this time. If charges were pressed, it didn't make the local press.

The group did not return to the venue

Friday 10th - Grand Pavilion. Withernsea, North Humberside

GRAND PAVILION WITHERNSEA
FRIDAY, 10th OCTOBER

SLADE

plus

SUPPORTING GROUP

and the

BIG M RECORD ROADSHOW

DOORS OPEN 8-30 P.M.   DANCING 9-00 P.M. TO 1-00 A.M.
Tickets £3   at the door £3-25

Tickets available from
Vales Newsagency, Music Shop, and The Grand Pavilion, Withernsea
...s0 at Gough & Davy, Saville Street, Hull
C Y M S Fernsway for tickets plus bus fares

Saturday 11th – University Great Hall, Richmond Rd, Bradford.

Monday 13th - Shoulder Of Mutton, Hardstoft, Derbyshire.

The crew turned up to this venue and were horrified to find that it was in the large detached rear function room of a country pub. The power supply was not adequate to power the group's PA and equipment, so a workaround had to be found quickly.

The group played in the function room to the right in this photo.

The group set up with their backs to the wall on the left and an almost floor level stage. A lighting gantry was put across the front of the stage as a barrier.

Wednesday 15th - University. Bridges Hall, Whiteknights Rd, Reading

Thursday 16th - Palais - Nottingham (cancelled)

Friday 17th - Pavilion, West Runton near Cromer, Norfolk
Support: Straight 8

Saturday 18th - Thames Polytechnic, Calderwood Street, Woolwich, London S.E.18

Sunday 19th - Lyceum Ballroom - London
Support: U2 / Discharge.

U2 weren't on the poster because The Last Words pulled out and U2 were picked up at the last minute.

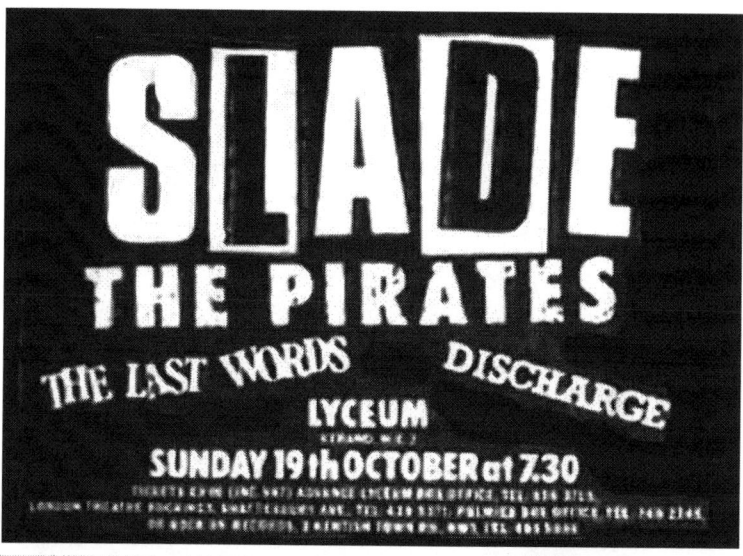

NODDY HOLDER gives Jim Lea a good bollocking

Slade/U2/Discharge
Lyceum

EUPHORIA, EXCITEMENT, acclaim, celebration — you name it, Slade commanded it tonight, roaring out of the swirling mists of time like conquering heroes returning to their native land.

'Retrogression' you scream, 'Bollox' I say, Slade were by far the punkiest band on the bill, but then the opposition weren't that hot...

Discharge oozed on first with all the grace and appeal of a syphilitic sore. Crassland refugees from grim old Stoke and frontline heroes of the even grimmer underground-punk mentality, Discharge suppurated a series of painful bursts of indistinguishable noise totally bereft of such essentials as choons and singalong choruses.

If it weren't for the fact that they threw in a few mumbles between songs I'd have been convinced they were playing one long-winded 40 minute concept number, doubtless dedicated to the destruction of four years of musical progress. Natch the smattering of Crass fans present loved every pustulent minute and the band encored on the strength of two farts and a cough down the front.

U2 came as a brief relief, sounding initially so much more positive than all that puerile pretend punk. But the magic soon wore thin as the cracks beneath the band's polished edifice became more and more apparent. Firstly, the newer material confirmed impressions that U2 are letting their pretentions run away with them, moving from the joyous pop gems that made their initial appearances so refreshing to tedious drawn-out yawns that even The Edge's often breath-taking fretwork fluency couldn't compensate for. And secondly Bono's glum, self-satisfied pronouncements became increasingly offensive as the night progressed. It seemed like he's beginning to believe the messianic treatment he's getting from the self-styled radical press — a real cotton wool job that lets him get away with outrageous nonsense, eg advocating Adam and Eve over Darwin, without being pulled up about it. Underneath the glittery surface U2 would appear to be nurturing some severely unhealthy elements...

Which is more than can be said for Slade, who presented one of the most pleasurable hours of yob-rock it's been my pleasure to 'oi-oi' to this year. The atmosphere had enough electricity to supply the domestic power needs of the USA for five years — the crowd was like a huge slice of the Kop 80 minutes into a 5-0 trashing — and Slade fed off it growing huger and more manic before our very eyes.

Honestly, I'd put money on it that this ain't the same band I watched striving rather desperately at the MM last year. It's as if the Reading triumph and the Top Fifty EP has pumped 'em full of new adrenalin and energy and confidence because the stage literally exploded in a mass of smoke bombs, silly trousers, toppers, bowlers, whooping and a-wailing and other expressions of purest glee.

I must admit I'd only come along to see the old classics — 'Everyday', 'Take Me Back 'Ome', 'Cum On Feel The Noize', 'Gudbye T' Jane', 'Mamma Weer All Crazee Now', 'Get Down And Get With It' et al — but like the old one goes nostalgia ain't what it used to be and before I knew it I was quite frankly swept off my feet by the sheer hard-rocking power of the reborn band.

The new Slade hit with the power of an out of control subway train putting most of the much-mooted NWOBHM to shame. 'Night Starvation' is a case in point, possessing more balls than a bingo caller and featuring Jimmy and Dave pogoing goofily along to its punky pace. Other highlights had to include the arms-in-air-with-imaginary-scarf classic 'Everyday' and the show-stealing (relative) newie 'The Wheels Ain't Coming Down', and as encore justifiably followed encore the evening dissolved in my memory as a gorgeous celebration of high energy entertainment, random football chants and carefree singsonging. Sham were never this good at it...

GARRY BUSHELL

Wednesday 22nd
Rodange - Grande Duche Du Luxembourg

Thursday 23rd
Salle Culturelle de Quiverain. Rue De L' Abatoir, Quievrain

Friday 24th
Poperinge
Saturday 25th
Lessines - Place D'Houraine ,Belgium

Sunday 26th
Ancienne Belgique, Talent Gaddress, 15, Rue De Pierres

Noddy startete Comeback in Reading

Dave macht die Show bei Slade

Beim englischen Pop-Festival in Reading überraschten Slade, die Mitte der 70er Jahre zu den Top-Bands gehörten, mit einem Super-Auftritt. Neben Gruppen wie Whitesnake, Rory Gallagher und Def Leppard sprangen sie ohne Ankündigung für Ozzy Osborne ein. Mit ihren Oldies „Cum on feel the Noize", und „Mama we're all crazy now" brachten sie die Fans zum Toben. In all den Jahren hat sich das Image von Noddy Holder, Jimmy Lea und Dave Hill genauso wenig wie ihre Songs verändert. Noddy trägt immer noch Federn am Hut, Dave tobt in grellbunten Farben auf Schleichsohlen über die Bretter, und Jimmy verrenkt sich zu gekonnten Gitarrensoli. In Kürze planen Slade wieder eine Europa-Tournee. Neueste Single: „You have to be a Hustler if you wanna get on".

Thursday 30th
Rotters Club, Silver Street, Doncaster

```
Silver St.     ROTTERS      Tel. 0302
Doncaster                       27448
```

PORTERHOUSE PROMOTIONS PRESENT—
★ TONIGHT ★ — TUESDAY, 30th SEPTEMBER
SLADE
Plus **JOAN JETT** (ex Runaways)
ADVANCE TICKETS £2.50

WEDNESDAY, 1st OCTOBER
THE SKIDS
Plus **THE BOOKS**
ADVANCE TICKETS £2.50.

TICKETS FROM ROTTERS, FOX'S, BARKER & WIGFALLS
Must be over 18 years of age.
NO DRESS RESTRICTIONS. NO MEMBERSHIP REQUIRED

NOVEMBER 1980

WELL SLADE!

★ Four years after the last rites were pronounced on Slade's meteoric chart career, the original "yob" rockers have returned from the dead.

With "Alive At Reading," the band who shot to fame in the early '70s with hits like Cum On Feel The Noize and Mama We'er All Crazee Now, have made a comeback right out of the blue.

But despite their disappearance from the public eye lead singer Noddy Holder says that the band have never really been away.

"We've been working as hard as ever since we dropped out of the charts," says Noddy, 30.

HAPPY

"We played at the heavy metal festival at Reading this year we got an incredible response—and this hit is the result."

Noddy still lives in his home town of Wolverhampton as does guitarist Dave Hill and bassist Jim Lea.

"This is where all my friends live and I'd never move away," says Noddy. "I never even thought about it, even when we were at our peak.

"Now I'm married with two kids. Leeandra and I are very happy together."

Merry Xmas from Slade

SLADE, who've been enjoying a new lease of life since they stopped the show at the Reading Festival in August, have lined up an extensive pre-Christmas tour. It ties in with the release this weekend by Polydor of their 20-track greatest hits album 'Slade Smashers', which includes six chart-toppers ('Merry Xmas Everybody' among them). Confirmed dates and venues are:

Norwich Cromwells (November 27), **Bath** University (28), **London Woolwich** Thames Polytechnic (29), **Bournemouth** Winter Gardens (December 1), **Canterbury** Kent University (2), **Uxbridge** Brunel University (3), **Wakefield** Unity Hall (5), **Sunderland** Polytechnic (6), **Wolverhampton** Civic Hall (7), **Hardstoft** Shoulder of Mutton (8), **Hucknall** Miners Welfare (10), **Sheffield** Polytechnic (12), **Hull** City Hall (13), **Manchester** Rotters (15), **Colwyn Bay** Pavilion (16), **Liverpool** Brady's (18), **Ashford** Stour Centre (19), **Birmingham** Odeon (20), **Dunstable** Queensway Hall (21) and **Grimsby** Central Hall (22).

Slade smash out

SLADE, whose "Slade Smashers" greatest hits album is released on Friday this week, open a month of touring at the end of November.

They play Norwich Cromwells on November 27, then Bath University (November 28), London Thames Poly (29), Bournemouth Winter Gardens (December 1), Canterbury Kent University (2), Uxbridge Brunel University (3), Wakefield Unity Hall (5), Sunderland Poly (6), Wolverhampton Civic Hall (7), Hardstoft Shoulder of Mutton (8), Sheffield Poly (12), Hull City Hall (13), Manchester Rotters (15), Colwyn Bay Pavilion (16), Liverpool Bradys (18), Ashford Stour Centre (19); Birmingham Odeon (20) Dunstable Queensway (21) and Grimsby Central Hall (22).

Saturday 1st: Polygram release the greatest hits type compilation 'Slade Smashes, which will climb to number 21 in the charts. It contains some different versions of singles than those which were originally released.

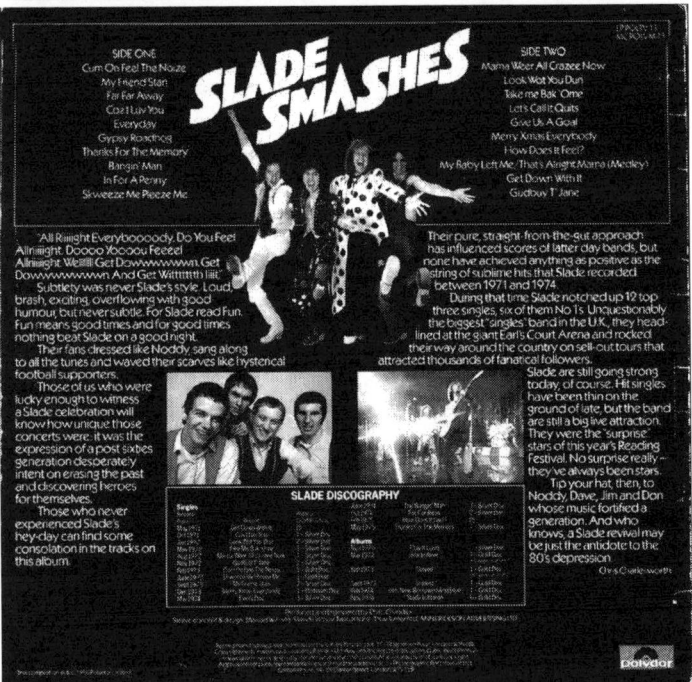

SLADE: 'Slade Smashes' (Polydor POLTV13)
By Mike Gardner

PEOPLE keep telling me there's a Slade revival on, but it's hard not to laugh. It's more than interesting to watch those who've seen them live attempt to convert those who keep their look of bemusement and incredulity intact during the discourse. It's also funny to watch the curious become fervant disciples whose faces light up at the mention of Slade. They're the ones who stumble across the truth, via the experience, that there is no Slade revival.

The word revival always implies that the band were redundant for a period between their "hey-day" and their "current resurgence" but Slade have remained constant throughout.

They slogged up and down the toilets and flea-pits of this country for five years before their first hit 'Get Down And Get With It' gave everybody the opportunity to realise that they are one of the best live attractions in this land.

Their aggressive, energetic and enthusiastic stage show was successfully translated into a string of raucous singles that celebrated the mythical rock 'n' roll spirit with a vengeance, songs like 'Mama Weer All Crazee Now', 'Cum On Feel The Noize', 'take Me Bak 'Ome', 'Gudbuy T'Jane' and the others contained on this 20 track precis of the time when Slade and the record buying public connected are the best reminders of the power some felt and other ignored.

Those who have realised the power of Slade will already have the majority of the songs on this collection. Those who have only recently caught up with the fact that Slade have remained constant and those that have reconnected with a fundamental lynch pin of that mess we call rock 'n' roll will find this set a useful but ultimately unsatisfying reminder of the joy and exuberance of the Birmingham quartet of Noddy, Jimmy, Don and Dave. Those who have yet to find out had better start here and then grasp the opportunity to "feel the noize" at the first chance. + + + + ½

DAILY EXPRESS Thursday November 6 1980

ANNE Nightingale COVERING THE POP SCENE

An early Christmas makes Slade merry again

ONLY SLADE could have done it ... persuade 80,000 hard-core heavy metal fans to sing "Merry Christmas Everybody" in the middle of August.

It happened at this year's Reading Festival, where Slade stormed the stage and stole the three-day show.

The four-strong group have been the forgotten men of rock 'n' roll for the past four years. In the early 'seventies, their football-chanting, stomping, rasping songs made them the idols of the original skinhead era and gave them 20 hits, including six number ones.

Then came their decline. Slade's last hit was in 1976 — a song called "Let's Call It Quits." Which seemed an apt title. The group left Britain for two years and many believed that Slade, together since 1968, had broken up.

Noddy Holder, whose vocal chords resemble a megaphone, is philosophic: "Having been out of Britain, in America, we expected to have to start again on the bottom rung of the ladder when we came back.

"In fact, we've never stopped working. It's a case of necessity — we're not millionaires."

In their last four hit-less years, Slade have still been knocking 'em for six at universities, colleges and clubs. "We'll play anywhere — Newcastle one night, Swansea the next," says Holder.

Now Slade are back in the lower reaches of the singles chart with a live recording of part of their stunning performance at Reading.

"We weren't even billed to appear," said Noddy. "We were booked as replacement to Ozzy Osbourne, at the last minute. There was a huge cheer when we went on stage. It was a hell of a break.

"Every band has a dip in their career at some stage. I remember seeing The Who playing at a ballroom in Wolverhampton some years ago. Things were not going that well for them. Then they brought out 'Tommy'— and never looked back."

This week, Polydor releases a Slade compilation album, "Slade's Smashers," which includes 20 of their original hits, like "Gudbuy to Jane" and "Mama Weer All Crazee Now."

And, of course, their luckiest song of all, "Merry Christmas Everybody" — No. 1 hit in 1973.

La punk nostalgique

SLADE
'Slade Smashes'
(Polystar POLTV 13) * * * * *

Or, the squalid truth about one man's misguided youth

I KNOW, I know, another five-star review. Seems that virtually every vinyl sweetmeat I weigh up these days is worthy of the ultimate accolade, but I kid you not chums, despite the gloomy doomy 'music is dead' attitudes promoted by various intensely boring manic depressive types I honestly believe that musically things have rarely been better.

Take a gander at some of the classic modern records that have seen the light of day these past few months — the Skids, the Jam, the Rejects, the Specials, Madness, Motorhead, Manners, — oi vay in a babylon breddren, talk about diamond wheezers. And at the same time not instead of musical progress but as a nice little bonus on the side, we've been treated to re-issues of some of the old time heroes who made my own teeny weeny days go with a grin and mucho din... Big Gal Glitter, the soon-come Judge Dread double and now this mighty meaty big and bouncy collection of twenty timeless Slade faves.

For once I'm speechless, well almost anyway, and it's only with near superhuman self restraint that I prevent these perspiring pinkies from tapping out the full horrorshow history of my Slade memories, from that initial encounter on the Eammon Andrews show blistering through 'Get Down And Get With It' with cropped-head conviction, through hundreds of backing track adolescent adventures, right up to undoubted chart supremacy and Earls Court mayhem with, I must confess, silly hat and cape flying in the wind.

All I'm gonna say is that as far as I can see this collection is a perfect reminder of the glories that were, marrying raucous rock and singalong pop in a superb celebration of unpretentious goodtimes.

They're all here, the rowdy faultless chart-toppers 'Cos I Luv You', 'Take Me Bak 'Ome', 'Mama Weer All Crazee Now', 'Skweeze Me Please Me', 'Merry Xmas Everybody' — ten silver discs, two gold discs, one platinum.

There's the mighty scarf-waving anthem 'Everyday' too, and the similarly moving homesick howsyafarver 'Far Far Away', not to mention the pre-Rejects football fave 'Give Us A Goal', the r'n'r circus medley 'My Baby Left Me/ That's Alright Mama', the stompin' stormer 'Get Down And Get With It', and even, whisper it, one or two I ain't so fond of like 'Thanks For The Memory' which makes me think maybe, just maybe, the rot was setting in even before the American failure. But they're just the exception that prove the proof of the pudding washes whiter.

Because what we're talking about here then, men, is a near miraculous disc that every home should have. And what's interesting is that recent live performances indicate that the band, despite their methusela-like antiquity still rock like good'uns and Noddy is still the same colourful clown with the prime primal power-lung scream, so maybe there's a chance that Slade'll become heroes again for a new generation...

For the moment however I don't give a monkey's toss about speculating and such like, all I wanna do is put this on again full blast and dodge the missiles from the ignorant barbarians who I'm forced to share this under-paid under-staffed office with.

ALRIGHTTTT EVERRRYBODYYY, DO YA FEEL ALRIGHT, (cont. ad nauseam)

GARRY BUSHELL

Smash and grab

SLADE: "Slade Smashes" (Polydor LPPOLTV13).

THE hilarious absurdity of it all won't be lost on Slade. Their sense of self-parody was never as overtly developed as that other priceless old trouper Gary Glitter, but they were, always invested with a glorious humour that must singlehandedly have carried them through some pretty grim times.

They'll be laughing themselves silly now at the sheer preposterousness of being despised, dismissed and literally spat out of contention during the mid/late Seventies; and then in 1980 suddenly being re-discovered and feted by the heavy metal brotherhood.

It further reinforces the old adage that if you hang about long enough it all comes round again. Personally, I'm unimpressed by the theory, but delighted by the circumstance — Slade have a damn sight more right to be heralded than, say, Bolan, especially as even in their heyday there were few critics with the guts to credit them for some great songs.

They were indelibly linked with glitter rock and teenybop, and most self-respecting journalists felt obliged to condemn all who sailed on the same ticket. It made me furious then and it makes me furious now.

I spent the early part of the Seventies schizophrenically delving into the history of the Copper Family with one hand and pumping a fist to Slade with the other, and if this album brings them belated acknowledgement of their rightful status in rock history then I'll be thrilled to my boots.

This is a wonderful collection of 20 tracks, whose value soars beyond mere nostalgia. Noddy Holder's voice — like John Lennon with a severe case of sandpapering — is as fearsome now as it was then, and Chas Chandler's production is sharp and full-blooded.

There was nothing tentative about Slade — if they rocked you were overwhelmed by the force, and when they moved into ballads there was no hiding behind strings or lush production. They were, and probably still are, the most honest band in the game. Here is insoluble evidence of their greatness, "Mama Weer All Crazee Now", "Gudbuy T'Jane", "Cum On Feel The Noize" et al. But it also proves that even during their commercial decline (triggered by misplaced ambition and spending too much time in America) some of the song they were producing were still classics — "The Bangin' Man", "How Does It Feel?", "Thanks For The Memory".

If 1980 has given us anything worthwhile it's creating a climate where you can walk into a store and buy a Slade greatest hits album and *still* look yourself in the mirror. — **COLIN IRWIN**.

Slade album and tour

Barry Plummer

SLADE, CURRENTLY enjoying a new wave of popularity, have a greatest hits album called 'Slade Smashers' out on Polydor this Friday (November 7) and play a British tour from the end of the month: (November 27) Cromwells, Norwich; (28) Bath University; (29) Thames Polytechnic; (December 1) Bournemouth Winter Gardens; (2) Kent University, Canterbury; (3) Brunel University, Uxbridge; (5) Unity Hall, Wakefield; (6) Sunderland Polytechnic; (7) Wolverhampton Civic Hall; (8) Shoulder Of Mutton, Hardstoft; (10) Miners' Welfare Hall, Hucknall; (12) Sheffield Polytechnic; (13) Hull City Hall; (15) Rotters Club, Manchester; (16) Colwyn Bay Pavilion; (18) Brady's, Liverpool; (19) Stour Centre, Ashford; (20) Birmingham Odeon; (21) Queensway, Dunstable; (22) Grimsby Central Hall.

5th: XMAS EARBENDER EP released on Cheapskate CHEAP 11 Merry Xmas everybody (Slade and Reading Choir) / Okey Cokey // Get Down And Get With It.

For fans, the prospect of having to purchase another disc with the Okey Cokey on it was not much short of horrifying. A year previously we hadn't seen the point of it and now here it was again, sandwiched between tracks from the Reading Festival and packaged similarly to the Reading EP. The group may have seen the point of this, but it did well to get to number 70 in the UK chart.

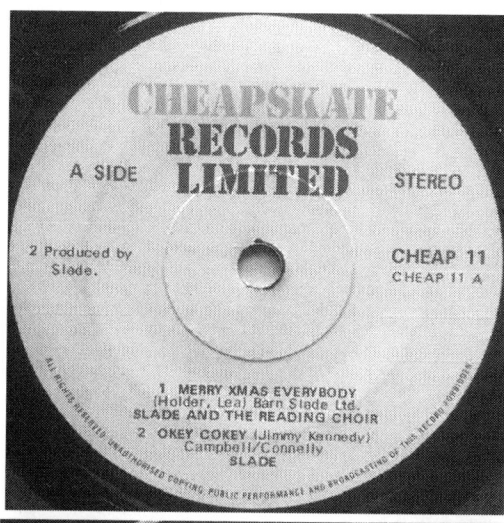

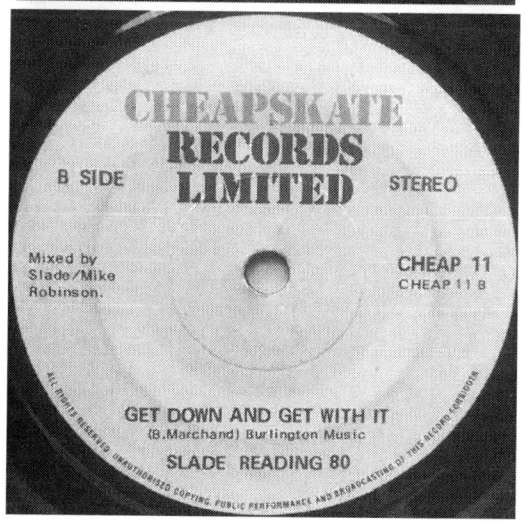

15th: SOUNDS feature on Slade...

BACK FROM THE DEAD

STEVE KEATON meets Noddy Holder and Jim Lea of Slade

THANKFULLY, some people just don't know when to give up. More six foot under than down and out, Slade have clawed their way back from Death's dark chart-file to currently stomp about town (platform boots a-glinting) with alarming vigour. The band that time forgot.

Oh Nod, forgive me for I have sinned, carelessly packing you off to has-been limbo. Flail me and be done.

Their legacy of course is considerable. Arguably the finest singles band of the early seventies, certainly one of the most influential, they gave birth to a rowdy brood of classic tracks. Each and every one complemented by memorable telly spots.

How I remember teetering about like an idiot to 'Mamma weer all crazee now', 'Cum on feel the noize' and 'Gudbye t'Jane' to name but three. Oh, for the days when a mirrored top hat was the height of street level elegance . . .

Eventually conquered peaks began to crumble under the weight of ambitions. A movie, 'Slade In Flame' was released — maybe the Scala will dig it out and refresh our memories? — and the decision to invade America taken. Like a row of teeth out at a Rejects' gig, they flew out of our lives. The end of an era. Supersonic died and Top Of The Pops was never the same again. Pause to wipe away the tears.

Meanwhile, back in the States, Slade were working their loons off. Two years of hard graft reaped precious few rewards. They came home in seventy seven just as the punk rebellion gobbed to its heights. The boys disembarked at Heathrow as an anachronism, no hero's welcome, just more hard graft.

Then bingo! A triumph at the Reading festival and the consequent release of the live at Reading EP featuring the smashing 'When I'm Dancing I Ain't Fighting' —

sledgehammer pop in the grand old tradition. A sparkling gig at the Lyceum was all I needed to be convinced that Slade were very much alive and well and on top form. So much for the potted history.

WRAPPED in a decidedly dodgy old blue duffel coat, his golfball peepers swivelling above equally blue bags, Noddy Holder ain't quite the hero I'd imagined. I was kinda hoping he'd greet me attired in all his silly stage togs, so to be confronted with this duffel coat . . . a bit of a downer as you can imagine.

Still, the man himself was bright and cheery, as was the wiry Jimmy Lea. Unfortunately drummer Don Powell and ace guitarist Dave Hill couldn't make the trip, intrigues up Wolverhampton way and all that, so I was denied the chance to ask really important stuff like 'Why does Dave persist with that truly hideous hair style?' and other burning issues. Thus limited I asked Nod (Neville really, amazing eh?) if they were getting a trifle desperate before the Reading break?

"No, it wasn't a matter of desperation," he declares, finally shedding said duffel coat, much to my relief.

"When we came back from the States the whole music scene had changed. It was a case of starting on the bottom rung of the ladder and working our way up again, which is what we set about to do really. Just slumming it around, doing gigs everywhere and anywhere. Not only in Britain but in Europe as well, making people aware that we hadn't split up and weren't sunning ourselves in the Bahamas. We've been working solid since the hit records stopped, always on the road.

"When we returned we were in a heavy vein, the album released then, 'Whatever happened to Slade' was a heavy album, and it didn't mean anything then. It was very Americanised. Totally out of context to what was going on at the time. If it was released now it would be in vogue because it's a heavy metal orientated LP."

Were you completely unaware of the developments over here then?

"No not really. We knew that there had been changes here — we'd read the papers. But you'd never hear any of the music on American radio. We were thinking, 'Who are these bands? What sort of music is it?' We got back and turned on the radio and its was like a revelation to us. Good God, what's happening?! It was a totally different feeling. We might as well have been in Japan."

The band took a year off then, to assess their own situation, finally lured back to the boards for a gig in Germany. That was quickly followed by one at Reading university.

"When we did that — Fantastic! We thought, 'Crike' if we can go down like that, let's do more gigs. And that's what we've been doing ever since."

Things weren't that simple though. It was hardly hip to be a Slade booster then. It seemed people just didn't want to know.

"The radio at the time just wouldn't play us. Now Nod and I can write some good tunes, but whatever went they wouldn't touch us. It was all to do with fashion. You can't be bitter about it, we understand it. We realised that the name Slade was uncool; we knew we had to overcome our own name and people's preconceived ideas as to what the band was about.

"It's taken us two years to overcome that hurdle . . . But we had to do that the first time round as well. People then used to associate the name Slade with the skinhead image. But we did it then and we'll do it now.

134

IT WAS in fact a lucky fluke that won the group the Reading spot. If it wasn't for a certain ex-Sab, Noddy and the rest might still be slogging around the country unnoticed, as the singer explains.

"Well, Ozzy Osbourne's band pulled out three days before the show and so they asked us to do it. We weren't on any of the billings or anything, we just stepped into Ozzy's place. We hadn't been on the road for two months. We just got a quick rehearsal together and went on. It hasn't changed to us since then but it certainly opened people's eyes. They're aware of us again."

"It was rather funny really," continues Jim, "We rolled up to Reading in our Ford Granada, we got sent to the public car park. We got all our guitars and cases and that out of the car and off we went struggling through the crowd. When we got to the artists enclosure we found that we didn't have our backstage passes, so there we were asking if we could come in. And stretching off behind us was a whole line of Rolls Royces.

"Now Whitesnake rolling up in a Rolls Royce you expect, being top of the bill. But everyone had one, the whole bill! And there's us with twenty hit records under our belt struggling through the dust.

"That's the way it's always been with us. The story of our lives, everything around us always falls apart. We've never been able to be cool. God, we've tried. I'm afraid we'll always be uncool. We felt like the outsiders going to Reading, but when we got backstage everyone started asking us for our autographs. We felt good then, that's when we knew we were in with a bloody good chance. We never die on stage either. Been around too long. We knew exactly what we were going to do, never had any problems with audiences."

The entire show was recorded by the BBC for broadcasting on the Friday rock show. Forty-five minutes of Slades set was aired. "We just had to release something from it, we had so many requests."

'When I'm dancing' and 'Born to be wild' were the selected songs, an arrangement was struck with the Beeb and the EP appeared on Jim Lea's own Cheapskate records label. It's currently jostling around the top forty as well as making a fleeting though high appearance in our own HM chart. It deserves your attention.

MEANWHILE Polydor are releasing a 'Slade Smashes' compilation invaluable for wretches like me who no longer possess the originals. I asked Nod if he was at all depressed at this preoccupation with past glories?

"Depressed? No. This compilation will be great for the fans, a chance to get all the hits on one record. But we don't relate to them in the same way any more, the way we play them now is bugger all like the records anyway."

Jim: "I didn't even like some of those old ones. We all hated 'Gudbye t'Jane' when we made it, it was knocked up in half hour at the end of one of our studio sessions. The same for our second single, 'Cos I love you'. It was namby-pamby to us, a throwaway for an album. It shot to number one in two weeks and we thought, 'What a pile of shit!' It was so wet.

"But they were good times. The success never changed us, because this band just doesn't have an ego — except for Dave. I remember there was this great rivalry between us and Bolan. We used to sit in the TOTP dressing room getting powdered up, with the Osmonds waiting behind us, and everyone was taking the piss out of one another. We would come out of the Beeb and there would be all these fans after autographs and stuff. Chicks would come up to Marc and say, 'Are you Marc Bolan? Ain't you fat.'

The duo chuckle happily at the memory.

"And now we're having to live down our success. Y'know it's much harder to make it the second time around. We've never, ever considered splitting up because we know that at the end of the day we can walk on stage and blow any fucker off — and that's what it all comes down to in the end.

"And that goes right back to the beginning. Like when we were skins we were outlawed, it was really bad then. No gigs, no radioplay, nothing. But we survived because we went to places like universities and that and tore the joints apart; not a skinhead in sight in the audience, it was all long haired hippies in those days.

"We just need people to see us at face value, see? Exactly the same as they did at Lincoln or Reading. They didn't fork out their ticket money to see us at those gigs, but once they did see us they accepted us for what we were and enjoyed it . . . and that's all we've ever been here for."

Thursday 27th - Cromwell Club, Edward Street, Norwich

Friday 28th - Bath University. Claverton Down, Bath
Support: The Drill

Review:
It seems that most people who've never seen Slade onstage would rather take a holiday in Siberia than make the effort. Slade are regarded as denizens of the pre-punk era who made music without – horrors! – a Message, in the naïve belief that music could be fun on its own.

People who have seen Slade can be excused a certain amount of smugness, but then, Slade don't have a name to live up to as much as they did, so the element of surprise works in their favour. The reason? Simple. Slade songs aren't bits of background that worm into your consciousness, they aren't meaningful expressions of sociological philosophy, or clever computer chords.

They are though, basic anthems of British rock at its purest and best: totally unpretentious, uncompromising and most of all, danceable.

Fred Williams
Sounds

Saturday 29th - Thames Poly. Calderwood St, Woolwich, London
Support: Taurus / The Drill

Thames Poly
Woolwich, SE18. 01-855 0618/9

SLADE
+ TAURUS + THE DRILL
Saturday November 29th

Open to Non-Students
Tickets: £2.50 in advance

Licenced Bar
£3.00 on door

DECEMBER 1980
Monday 1st - Winter Gardens, Exeter Road, Bournemouth - Taurus - The Drill

Tuesday 2nd
Darwin College. University of Kent, Canterbury.

Wednesday 3rd
Kingdom Room, Brunel University, Uxbridge
Support: Taurus / The Drill

BRUNEL UNIVERSITY STUDENTS UNION
Presents
In The Kingdom Room,
Kingston Lane, Uxbridge

Friday 28th Nov.

AFTER THE FIRE
+ The Lasers
Adm. £2.00 8pm

Wed 3rd Dec.

SLADE
+ Taurus + The Drill
Adm. £2.50. Advance £2.75 door 8pm.

BRUNEL ENTS PRESENTS
IN THE KINGDOM ROOM

SLADE
plus Support
Wednesday, 3rd Dec., 1980

Adv. £2.50   Door £2.75

Friday 5th
Unity Hall. Westgate, Wakefield
Support: Taurus / The Drill

Unity Hall during an extensive refurbishment. A sizeable venue.

Saturday 6th
The Polytechnic. Wearmouth Hall, Chester Rd, Sunderland
(CANCELLED – JIM LEA UNWELL)

S.P.S.U. PRESENTS

SLADE

IN CONCERT
AT WEARMOUTH HALL
SATURDAY 6TH DEC. 1980
7 P.M.   LATE BAR

TICKETS £2.50 MEMBERS IN ADVANCE
£3.00 NON-MEMBERS
£3.00 ON THE DOOR

Sunday 7th - Civic Hall. North St, Wolverhampton Support: The Drill

Monday 8th Shoulder Of Mutton, Hardstoft. Support: Taurus

Wednesday 10th:
The Hucknall And Linby Miners Welfare Club. Portland Rd, Hucknall.

Radio Trent recorded the gig for a later broadcast. The complete show was included in the All The World Is A Stage Live Box, released in September 2022.

Sick pop star rocks on

Slade bass player Jimmy Lea staggered from his sick bed, despite "feeling like death", to play for the group's Wolverhampton fans at the civic hall last night.

And the ecstatic crowd could hardly have guessed that Lea had been vomiting blood prior to what friends said was one of their finest shows for ages.

Jimmy was taken ill during Friday's show at Wakefield, and although he finished the concert he was sick for an hour and a half afterwards.

The group took him back to their motel, but he was taken ill in the middle of the night and had to go to hospital, where he was given injections of antibiotics.

He was so ill that Saturday's scheduled show at Sunderland, was cancelled, and it was thought that Wolverhampton's concert would also have to be called off.

But the group had been looking forward to their home town show so much that Jimmy decided he would try to do the concert if possible.

His wife Louise said today: "He looked like death warmed up yesterday, but he went to the hospital and got a booster injection which helped a bit. You couldn't tell by looking at him on stage that he was ill.

HUCKNALL/LINBY MINERS' JOINT WELFARE
PORTLAND ROAD, HUCKNALL
Tel. Nottingham 632119 or 630313

Notice to members

Main Hall

Friday, December 5th
Popular dance to
'ROOKIE'
Group

Cabaret and Bingo
NEIL GRANT
Brilliant Vocalist
SOYA & BEAN
Comedy Duo
Admission Free

Sunday, December 7
Cabaret and Bingo
HOJO
Group
Admission Free

Monday, December 8
PRIVATE FUNCTION

Tuesday, December 9
PRIVATE FUNCTION

Wednesday,
December 10
PRIVATE FUNCTION

Thursday, December 11
PRIVATE FUNCTION

Welbeck Suite

Friday, December 5th
OVER 18's DISCO
Admission £1

Saturday, December 6
PRIVATE FUNCTION

Sunday, December 7
Nashville Sound
Country and Western
Club
COUNTRY SNACK
Promising Band
Admission £1

Monday, December 8
OLD TIME AND
MODERN SEQUENCE
DANCE
Admission 30p

Tuesday, December 9
POPULAR (50/50)
DANCE
Admission 30p

Wednesday,
December 10
JUDO CLUB

Thursday, December 11
PRIVATE FUNCTION

> H. L. M. W. BAND
> present
> AT THE PIT ROCK VENUE
> HUCKNALL/LINBY MINERS' WELFARE
>
> # SLADE
>
> PLUS SUPPORT
> on WEDNESDAY, 10th DECEMBER, 1980
> 7.30 p.m. Start
>
> No Under 18's
> TICKETS £3.00
>
> N.º 004

Thursday 11th – University, Leicester.

This show was broadcast live on the Mike Read Show on BBC Radio 1. The group rearranged their song list for the radio broadcast and the power failed during their Christmas song (fortunately at the very end of it) and the live broadcast ended in confusion. The audience had a number of casualties from heat exhaustion.

Slayed—by the heat

AN atmosphere close to mass hysteria was generated at a concert by rock group Slade in Leicester University's Queen's Hall last night, broadcast on Radio One.

Hailed by even seasoned rock fans as the best concert ever seen in Leicester, it attracted an audience described by one observer as "suicidal".

Almost 1,500 people crushed into the hall in temperatures of 100F plus, filling it to capacity.

More than 100 young people suffering from heat exhaustion littered the corridors and there were fears that somebody might suffer a stroke or be seriously injured in the "tidal wave" crush.

Many girls were carried out dazed while some were physically sick from the heat.

Andrew Marston, a 22-year-old veteran of heavy metal concerts, traditionally extremely loud and hot affairs was one of those who had to leave the hall. He described what happened. "It looked like World War Three had been declared. There were bodies everywhere."

Slade bassist Jim Lea is used to this sort of reaction.

One of the four Wolverhampton musicians comprising Slade, he said he had felt ill at one point during the show.

ENTS spokesman Paul Davies, who organised the concert in conjunction with the Radio One Roadshow and the students' own Christmas Ball, said: "I didn't see any mass hysteria. It was very hot. There was condensation everywhere and the hall was so packed we couldn't get to the windows to open them."

We gonna rock ya / Dizzy Mama / When I'm Dancin' I ain't fightin' / Take Me Bak 'Ome / The Wheels Ain't Comin' Down / Everyday / Gudbuy T'Jane / You'll Never Walk Alone / Merry Xmas Everybody.

Friday 12th - Phoenix Building, The Polytechnic, Pond St, Sheffield.

№ 0534

Sheffield City Polytechnic
Union of Students ENTS

presents

Graduation Gala with SLADE

✚ SUPPORT

FRIDAY, 12 DECEMBER, 1980

SMART DRESS, please   NO JEANS   BAR 'til 2.00 am
Members and bona fide guests only   No re-admission   R.O.A.R.
This portion to be retained

Slade
Sheffield City Polytechnic

CUM On Feel The Noize, Slade are back and still as subtle as the proverbial flying mallet.

They have dusted down their string of seventies' hits and presented them in a heavy metal showcase.

There's more than a touch of the football terraces as toilet rolls are hurled over the stage and the heaving masses are invited to join in with "You'll Never Walk Alone."

Not my cup of half-time Bovril, but the packed Poly seemed well and truly Slayed.

The highlight of the evening was the "Merry Christmas" encore — complete with Noddy Holder in Santa's outfit.

Saturday 13th - City Hall, Hull.
Support: Taurus - The Drill

Monday 15th - Rotters Club. Oxford St ,Manchester.

Nº 912

OXFORD STREET, MANCHESTER
Tel. 061-236-4934

MONDAY, 15th DECEMBER Open 7 p.m. - 12 midnight
Guests on stage 8 p.m.

Porterhouse Promotions Present

SLADE
PLUS
SPECIAL GUESTS

Tickets £2.50 in advance

Must be over 18 years of age

THE MANAGEMENT RESERVE THE RIGHT TO REFUSE ADMISSION

PORTERHOUSE PROMOTIONS Presents

Tuesday 9th Dec
XTC
+ Special guests at
Liverpool Rotters
Tel 051 709 0771
Adv tickets £2.50

Sunday 14th Dec
DEF LEPPARD +
Special guests at
Doncaster Rotters
Tel.
0302 27448
Adv. £2.50

SLADE
+ Special guests at
Manchester Rotters
Tel 061 236 4934
Adv £2.50

For times & ticket outlets see
local press. Must be over 18
years of age. No dress
restrictions. No membership
required

OXFORD ST.
MANCHESTER
ROTTERS
TEL 061
236 4934

PORTERHOUSE PROMOTIONS PRESENT
MONDAY 15th DECEMBER
DOORS OPEN 7pm - 12 MIDNIGHT
SUPPORT BAND ON STAGE 8p.m.

SLADE

PLUS SPECIAL GUESTS
ADVANCE TICKETS £2.50
Tickets from Rotters, Virgin, Paperchase
HMV Record Stores
MUST BE OVER 18 YEARS OF AGE
NO DRESS RESTRICTIONS   NO MEMBERSHIP REQUIRED

Tuesday 16th - Dixieland Showbar, Abergele Rd, Colwyn Bay, Wales.
Support: Taurus / The Drill

Thursday 18th - Brady's Club. 9 -21 Matthew St, Liverpool

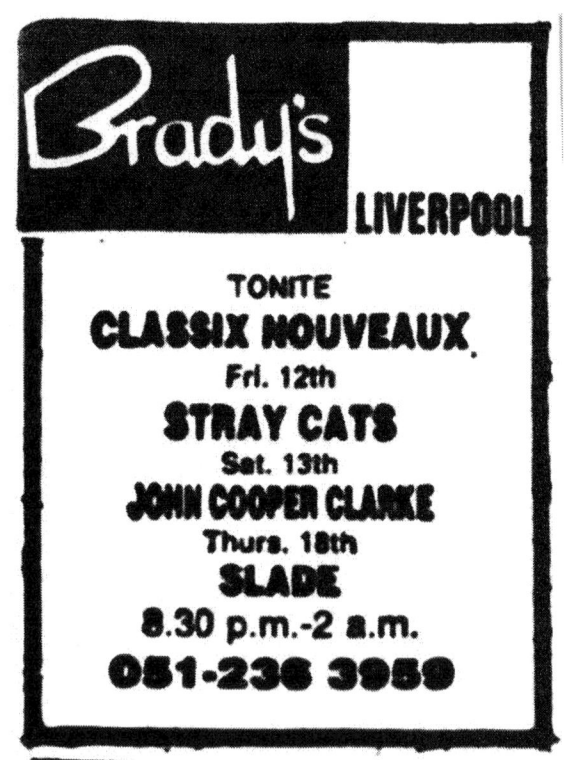

Friday 19th - Stour Centre. Tannery Lane. Ashford
Support: The Drill

Fri 19th Dec STOUR CENTRE, ASHFORD, KENT

WITH SPECIAL GUESTS OF THE CAROLINE ROADSHOW

SLADE + The Drill

Doors Open 7.30 Adm £2.50

Saturday 20th - Odeon. New Street, Birmingham.
Support: The Drill

Slade in the aisles

**Slade
Odeon, New Street,
Birmingham.**

Slade got with it — and gave Birmingham fans a night to remember at the weekend.

No one who watched their Christmas bonanza at the Odeon could have doubted that the former chart-toppers are on their way back with a vengeance.

The fans started the night at fever pitch and Noddy took them from strength to strength in a rip-roaring set that did not lose pace for a second.

The jubilant football-crowd atmosphere continued even after the lights went up, with Noddy setting the crowd singing along to the cinema muzak.

No one could grudge the Wolverhampton outfit their sensational come-back reception.

Having slogged for four years through the small club circuit since their fall from favour, they deserve it for sheer determination alone.

Some of the rawest edges have been rubbed off in that time — but Slade are still sticking basically to their raucous, gutsy, over-the-top brand of rock.

And despite the blow to their pride, they have not lost an ounce of enthusiasm for what they are doing.

Classics like *Gudbye t Jane* and *Merry Christmas* inevitably set the sell-out crowd jumping the hardest — but they could hardly have asked for a better reaction to any of their numbers.

JACKIE BAILEY

SLADE AT THE ODEON THEATRE, NEW STREET, BIRMINGHAM

The Wolverhampton wonders returned to Birmingham on Saturday night on yet another comeback trail with a typically aggressive and rather old-fashioned show – little has changed for the heavy rockers.

Their fans have not altered, either. Packed to the walls they greeted their heroes with a tidal wave of song and chant – it was the unquestioning loyalty normally reserved for football teams.

The lads began the show with an air of mystery with dark covers hiding... we didn't know what. Tiers of loudspeakers towered over the scene: the bots planned to bounce back with a bang, that much was clear.

The lights went down, the covers came off. Slade started playing in the dark. Then lo, there was dazzling light and the big surprise of the night was further stacks of equipment and guitarist Dave Hill dressed like Ragtime Cowboy Joe.

Of such elementary theatre was the show comprised, but then subtlety was never the band's forte. The volume was fierce, dry ice fog billowed incessantly, strobe lights flickered, globe lights glittered and balloons hovered overhead.

Slade took all of one second to settle down, but then, given their uncomplicated style – a musical equivalent to digging hoiles in the road with pneumatic drills – it is not surprising. Hits like Mama Weer All Crazee Now and Take Me Bak 'Ome (their spelling, not mine) were mixed with new numbers like The Wheels Ain't Coming Down, all screeched out by Noddy Holder in fine rabble-rousing form.

Slade came on late and left early – less than 45 minutes – but naturally returned for several long encores and for 2,600 contented fans, Slade wuz 'ere.

Jonathan Daumler-Ford
Birmingham Evening Mail

Slade comeback—on home ground

Black Country pop stars Slade are coming back home in their first major concert tour in years.

The group, which had more than 20 hit singles, is playing concerts in Wolverhampton and Birmingham in a nationwide comeback attempt.

It is now five years since the band had its last Top Ten single after years of being one of Britain's biggest pop attractions.

Now, after playing cabarets and clubs, they are returning to the big concert halls to win back the fans.

The comeback follows a surprise success at the giant Reading Festival — and the Black Country band believe it can be a success all over again.

Concerts at Wolverhampton Civic Hall on December 7 and Birmingham Odeon on December 20 are part of a special Christmas comeback tour.

Record company chiefs plan to release Slade's "greatest hits" album to help boost ticket sales.

Walsall-born singer Noddy Holder, who recently put his £98,000 Sutton bungalow up for sale, said: "I think we were too successful to start with. Our records went to No 1. as soon as they were released. We won gold awards and couldn't do any wrong."

NEW STREET BIRMINGHAM B2 4NU
Tel: 021-643-6101
SAE With All Postal Bookings Please

TONIGHT (FRIDAY) AT 8.00 p.m.
Adrian Hopkins presents
STEELEYE SPAN
CANIS MAJOR
£4.00 £3.00 £2.00

TOMORROW (SATURDAY) AT 7.30 p.m.
Straight Music presents
ULTRAVOX
£3.00 £2.50 £2.00

Sunday, December 7 at 7.30 p.m.
Adrian Hopkins presents
BUDGIE
WHITE SPIRIT
TROUBLESHOOTER
All Tickets £2

Monday, December 8 at 7.30 p.m.
Wall to Wall Stage Shows presents The Frontier Tour plus Ant Music Review starring
ADAM & THE ANTS
Plus GODS TOYS
£3.00 £2.50

Saturday, December 20 at 7.00 p.m.
M.C.P. presents
SLADE
THE DRILL
£3.25 £3.00 £2.75

Monday, January 26 at 7.30 p.m.
Adrian Hopkins presents
U.F.O.
Plus Support
£3.50 £3.00 £2.50

Wednesday, February 25 at 7.30 p.m.
Kennedy Street Enterprises present

Sunday 21st - Queensway Hall. Vernon Place, Dunstable
Support: The Drill

Monday 22nd - Central Hall. Duncombe Street, Grimsby
Support: The Drill

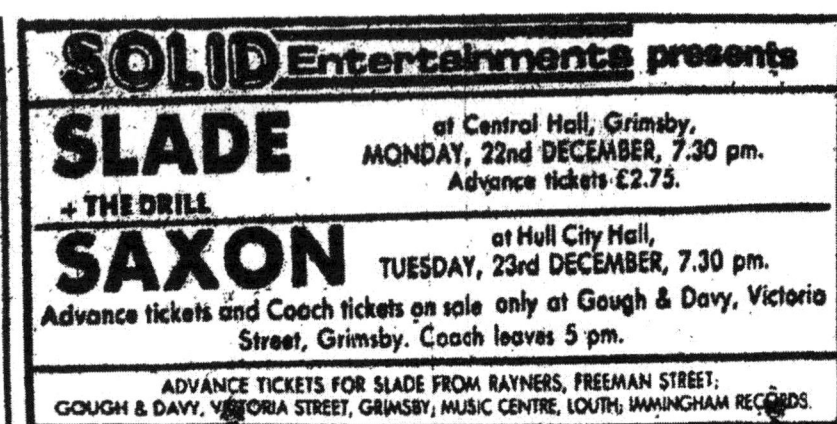

Tuesday 30th - Rotters Club. Silver Street, Doncaster

MOST INSPIRED COMEBACK OF THE YEAR

1. SLADE
2. JOHN LENNON
3. GARY GLITTER
4. David Bowie
5. Ultravox
6. Adam & The Ants
7. Bruce Springsteen
8. Ronald Reagan
9. Diana Ross
10. Ian Gillan

AUTHOR'S NOTE

This book has combined the years 1979 and 1980, because Slade were not visible for part of 1979 and 1980, until after the Reading Festival.

THANKS

There are a number of people who I would like to thank: The members of Slade. The Slade book writers. There are some great new books out there. The Slade website people. The 'From Roots To Boots' blog site, which is run by Michael Parker. The few people who actually answered my emails and messages, especially as I am so bad at using the internet. All the people who ran Slade Fan Club magazines – I have used parts of some *(but not entire)* interviews in this book. They are historically important.

I would like to sincerely thank Don Powell for putting his diary entries for these years online. I have quoted a couple of of his remarks from entries, as they are quite interesting and must reflect what life in the group was like. This copy of the book is a second edition which doesn't directly quote Don's diaries verbatim, due to copyright.

While doing my research I found a wealth of Slade websites and in a number of old magazines. No book would be the same without its reference material. Thank you to the writers for those articles, (for magazines which all seem to be sadly defunct these days). While some parts of the content may indeed have been available previously, it has never all been under one roof, so to speak. Most of the content is from the press archives where I seem to spend my daylight hours. I have credited some photos where possible. One website allowed use of photos providing the watermark remained.

Thanks to the people who offered publishing advice - it was very much appreciated. Nigel, Dee, Davey and Bernie for sage advice.

Love to Lisa.

Thank you to Lisa for setting this web page up for me:
www.facebook.com/TonyCharlesAuthor

BIBLIOGRAPHY

FEEL THE NOIZE.
Chris Charlesworth. Omnibus.

LOOK WOT I DUN
Lise Lyng Falkenberg.
Omnibus.

WHO'S CRAZEE NOW?
Noddy Holder / Lisa Verrico.
Ebury.

THE WORLD ACCORDING
TO NODDY HOLDER.
Noddy Holder. Constable.

SLADE
George Tremlett. Futura.

THE SLADE PAPERS
Music Sales Ltd.

BRAVO SCRAPBOOK
Rexpert Books.

CUM ON FEEL THE NOIZE
Alan G Parker and Steve Grantley

THE NOIZE Second Edition.
Chris Selby / Ian Edmundson.
Self-publish, Amazon.

SIX YEARS ON THE ROAD
Ian Edmundson.
Self-publish, Amazon.

SLADE IN FLAME
John Pigeon. Panther.

SO HERE IT IS.
Dave Hill. Unbound.

IMAGE RESTORATION

The gig advert images in these books are more often than not from press archives, and they are forty years OLD!! Some are damaged almost irreparably and some are nearly impossible to read.

You may not think of it when glancing through these books, but some of these images can take over an hour each to restore to a readable state. Some have actually taken a few attempts. They won't always be one hundred percent perfect, but I have tried my best. I'd like to thank a great Slade fan for invaluable advice. These books wouldn't have appeared without that help.

Books by TONY CHARLES in the SLADE YEAR BY YEAR series.

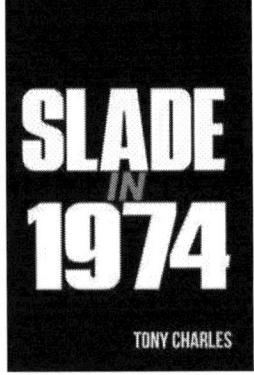

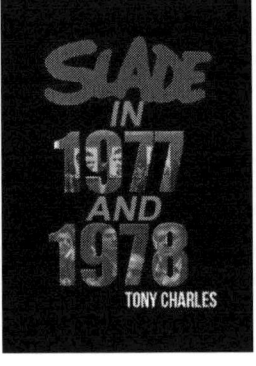

Watch This Space.....

TONY CHARLES

Tony Charles is the author of this series of Slade books, which aims to cover the period when Slade had a live career.

Married to the ever-patient Lisa and the proud father of two grown-up sons. When they fled to their own homes, to escape the sound of Tony's drums, the empty nest provided some office space and retirement allowed time to browse far-off newspaper archives via the internet and, to his amazement, books started to flow.

Formerly a gas fitter by trade, he has written pieces for a few hobbyist magazines over many years and having retired in 2020, now divides his time between a holiday flat in The Algarve with a really spotty internet connection and the family home in south London.

Tony also has a book on Queen in the works.

Printed in Great Britain
by Amazon